SOCIETY OF ILLUSTRATORS
51ST ANNUAL OF AMERICAN ILLUSTRATION

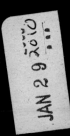

SOCIETY OF ILLUSTRATORS
51ST ANNUAL OF AMERICAN ILLUSTRATION

SI
51

FROM THE EXHIBITION HELD IN THE GALLERIES OF THE
MUSEUM OF AMERICAN ILLUSTRATION AT THE SOCIETY OF ILLUSTRATORS
128 EAST 63RD STREET, NEW YORK CITY
JANUARY 7 — MARCH 28, 2009

PUBLISHED BY SOCIETY OF ILLUSTRATORS AND COLLINS DESIGN

COLLINS DESIGN
An Imprint of HarperCollinsPublishers

ILLUSTRATORS 51
Society of Illustrators, Inc.
128 East 63rd Street, New York, NY 10065-7392
www.societyillustrators.org

FIRST PUBLISHED IN 2010 BY
Collins Design
An imprint of HarperCollins Publishers
10 East 53RD Street
New York, NY 10022
Tel: (212) 207-7000
Fax:(212) 207-7654
collinsdesign@harpercollins.com
www.harpercollins.com

DISTRIBUTED THROUGHOUT THE WORLD BY
HarperCollins Publishers
10 East 53RD Street
New York, NY 10022
Fax: (212) 207-7654

LIBRARY OF CONGRESS CONTROL NUMBER: 2009933889
ISBN: 9780061928000

EDITOR, Jill Bossert
BOOK AND JACKET DESIGN BY Erin Mayes and Simon Renwick, EmDash
JACKET COVER ILLUSTRATIONS BY Edel Rodriguez (front); Luc Melanson (back)

PHOTO CREDITS: Jury photos by Kevin Schneider

PRINTED IN CHINA
First printing, 2009

S I 5 I

TABLE OF CONTENTS

DENNIS DITTRICH

The Society's *Annual of American Illustration* is a pictorial record of what America is thinking. Information filtered through the mind of an illustrator serves to inform, entertain, and sell. Thousands of drawings make an animated movie; one can cause a protest march.

The rich variety of work in this volume represents the jury's best effort to choose, from some 6,000 entries, a representative cross section of the finest illustration produced within a year. The choices are based on the collective aesthetic of 42 professionals from the graphic arts community.

The annual book is a gold mine of pictures. For both students and professionals, it provides a way to measure ourselves as artists against our colleagues and predecessors. For over half a century, the Society's annual books have kept the bar high. Marching toward 100, we proudly present *Illustrators 51*. Enjoy!

DENNIS DITTRICH

Facing page: Portrait by Murray Tinkelman.

CHAIR'S MESSAGE
STEVEN GUARNACCIA

I can't think of a more interesting time to have chaired the annual exhibition. In the 51st year of the competitions, the field, and much of print culture, is at a crossroads. What a perfect moment to contemplate where we are and to peer into the future. Why are so many digital images sent to hang on the walls, even when an original exists? Will the day come when the art on the walls at the Society's shows will be seen solely on screen? Certainly one of the effects of the digital revolution is the sameness in size of most of the exhibited art, determined by the size of the scanner bed.

I was happy to preside over a competition this year that saw the paradox of an increase in entries while the field was supposedly in decline. While budgets are stagnant or worse, illustrators continue to make images that communicate to a wide audience. They continue to find new means of expression and outlets for themselves and their ideas. In many cases this means they take matters into their own hands, publishing their own books and creating their own products.

It's no news that we're living in an increasingly visual culture—one often based on drawn visuals, at that. *The New York Times Book Review* has taken to reviewing graphic novels alongside text-driven books, animated films are routinely up for Oscars, and video games are increasingly visually sophisticated.

It seems like just yesterday that word on the street was: Illustration Is Dead. The *AIGA Journal* published an article about it, the Draw conference hosted a panel about it, and illustrators sweated about it. Illustration has been pronounced dead many times in the last few years, when in fact it has been doing what it has always done: going about its business of adapting, mutating, serving the needs of new and varied clients and of young and adventurous visual artists. And it's the artists who have kept illustration alive. As the markets that illustration has traditionally served have been challenged, sometimes to within an inch of their lives, the unsinkable spirit of illustrators has remained buoyant. The need to make something, and in particular to make something that communicates to a wide audience, has sustained illustrators, even when

the field hasn't. Illustration's health has always depended on its ability to adapt to a variety of markets, and to take on a multiplicity of forms.

Illustration's purview used to be pretty easy to define. Traditionally, illustration accompanied a text, illuminating an article in a newspaper, magazine, or story in a children's book, or underscoring the copy in an ad. Now, illustration is as likely to take center stage. It has cut itself free, in many instances, from the constraints of reflecting a text, and it has therefore not been so easy to recognize where its boundaries are.

It used to be said that the difference between a fine artist and an illustrator was that an illustrator only worked when the phone rang. Could you really call yourself an illustrator if you toiled privately in your studio for no one's benefit but your own? If your work was printed nowhere and seen by no one—never mind that fine artists had been doing that for centuries. But the need to make things, to respond to the culture that stood illustrators in such good stead when times were flush, kept illustrators working even when the phones had stopped ringing. A new gallery-oriented illustrator was born, first in Los Angeles (where distinctions between high and low culture had never been very firmly drawn) and then in New York and elsewhere. And illustrators have also made forays into toy and product design, animation, graphic novels, and comics. These artists think like illustrators, are influenced by the same things illustrators have always been influenced by. In fact, many or most of these artists are illustrators, who have now re-imagined themselves, and in the process have created new audiences that share their enthusiasms and imagination. The field and its future have never looked so vibrant and vital.

I want to thank everyone who helped me bring the exhibitions into its second 50 years: the jurors, the past chairs, my former co-chair, Peter de Sève, and my current co-chair Nora Krug. I want to thank all the artists whose exceptional work continue to make the jurying process, with all of its technological changes, an exciting and surprising experience. And I especially want to thank Anelle Miller, the Society's director, for her support all along the way.

Facing page: Portrait by George Hardie.

Hall of Fame 2009

Since 1958, the Society of Illustrators has elected to its Hall of Fame artists recognized
for their "distinguished achievement in the art of illustration."
The list of previous winners is truly a "Who's Who" of illustration. Former presidents
of the Society meet annually to elect those who will be so honored.

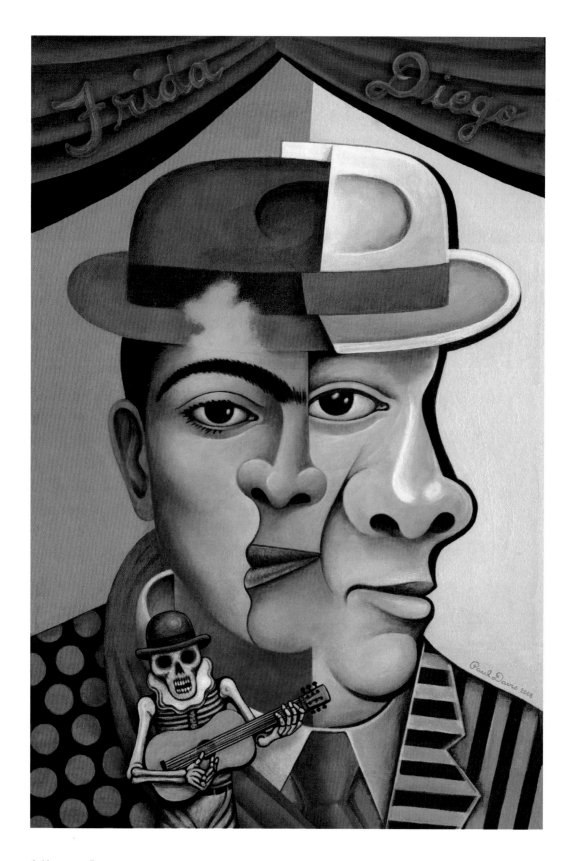

Paul Davis

[b. 1938]

Since he arrived in New York from Oklahoma in 1955 at the age of 17, Paul Davis's ambition has been to make exciting graphic images, a task at which he is considered to be a master. Although his portraits and landscapes have illustrated everything from books to restaurant walls, it is for his theater-related images that Davis is most famous. The theater, with its allegiance to energy and ideas, gave free reign to Davis's sense of humor, his critical intelligence, and his daring. "They're such a unique combination of glamour and power," said the director Mike Nichols. "They themselves are theater," Kurt Vonnegut wrote.

His landscapes are a hedge against loss. Davis, who was born in Centrahoma, Oklahoma, has a powerful feeling for the change in the landscape over his lifetime. "I've always had this thing about the vanishing West," he says. "I wanted to erase a lot of what was happening." The child of a Methodist minister, Davis moved eight times in his first 11 years. A roll call of the towns he passed through—Caddo, Jenks, Sulphur Springs, Great Falls, Hartshorne, Antlers—gives a sense of the blue highways the family followed as it crisscrossed between parsonages in Kansas, Arkansas, Montana, and Oklahoma. "I kept losing my environment, having to start over each time," Davis says. Drawing became his way of making a reality he could hold on to.

Davis also grew up around newspapers and type. His parents had met at the print shop at John Brown University in Siloam Springs, Arkansas. [His mother] Susan's father owned a Kansas newspaper, *The Bunker Hill Advertiser*. Later, she worked as a linotyper at her brother's newspaper, *The Ellis Review*. "I would watch them set type," Davis recalls. "I knew all this stuff—point size, typeface, leading, spacing ... all the subtleties of print." When his father read him the funny papers, "I would look at the way it was drawn. In *Pogo*, the type would change according to the character. The circus guy would start talking in circus letters, another would talk in Old English typeface. It blew me away."

"I read *The Saturday Evening Post* and the women's magazines and it seemed to me that those artists—Norman Rockwell, Stevan Dohanos, Jon Whitcomb, Al Buell, Coby Whitmore—were better than

anything else." By the time he was 15, Davis had decided on a career as a magazine illustrator. His family had moved to Tulsa, where he attended the Will Rogers High School. "If it hadn't been for that school, I would have never gotten out of Oklahoma," Davis says. "Hortense Bateholts was the Knute Rockne of art teachers. She instilled a lot of ambition in me. "The illustrators that interested me were those who cared more about painting, people like Fletcher Martin and Ben Stahl and Ben Shahn. There was something about them that was a lot more individual. I could see that it wasn't mainstream. I thought, well, there's a place for me."

Each year *Scholastic Magazine* awarded 150 art school scholarships to seniors; in 1955, Davis was one of the recipients. His choices included the Chicago Art Institute, the Philadelphia Museum School, Syracuse University, Pratt, and the School of Visual Arts in New York, which was only seven years old and still called the Cartoonists and Illustrators School. The latter appealed to him. "It wasn't very well known, but I had read about it in a comic book," Davis said.

His favorite artists were people like Saul Steinberg, André François, and Ronald Searle, all of whom fell under the category of cartoon artist. "I really wanted to be an illustrator but the other schools didn't mention illustration, just painting and drawing. What was being taught in the universities was abstraction." Davis also didn't like to draw rooms, buildings, or machines, because, as he said later, "They have too many flat lines ... I enjoyed making pictures of landscapes and animals and portraits. The unconscious elements that rose to the surface as I worked interested me most."

"It was hard work to come to New York to stay," Davis says. "But I was fascinated by it all." There followed a first marriage in 1959 to aspiring actress-singer Elise Hepburn, which produced his son John. In his third year [of art school], Davis had already sold a drawing to *Playboy*. He had also evolved a new, childlike style. "I threw away everything that I'd learned. My teachers, Phil Hays and George Tscherny, saw the potential in my experiments ... inspired by Klee, Miró, Picasso, de Kooning. I had been watching all the students. A lot could draw better. The one thing I could do was be more free."

By the time Davis joined forces with Joe Papp and the Public Theater in 1975—an association that would continue until Papp's death in 1991—he had already built up more than a decade's worth of magazine

Frida and Diego, 2008. Poster for a project organized by Gabriela Rodriguez to commemorate the creative relationship between Frida Kahlo and Diego Rivera. One hundred artists created posters for an exhibition in Mexico. All art courtesy of the artist.

TOP LEFT: *Big Apple Circus*, 1981. One of several commissioned posters I created for the group. My elder son John posed for the clown. TOP RIGHT: *Drinks Before Dinner*, 1978. One of 51 posters created for Joe Papp in a 19-year relationship. This play was written by E. L. Doctorow and directed by Mike Nichols. OPPOSITE: *Caroline, or Change*, 2004. Key advertising art for the musical written by Tony Kushner. The ad agency was Serino Coyne.

and book illustrations. In 1959, he became an assistant at Push Pin Studios. In 1963, Davis went solo. Over the next ten years he pioneered a much-imitated style. In a 1972 series of landscapes for Olivetti, he mythologized his Southwestern childhood. He also married, in 1965, former Push Pin colleague Myrna Mushkin, and their son Matthew was born in 1967.

Davis's direct dramatic style found startling expression in his heroic image of the Cuban leader Che Guevera (1967) for *The Evergreen Review*. The elegant image, which became emblematic of that era of American protest, was attacked; the office of the magazine was fire-bombed. "They gouged it with knives ... It scared me."

His poster, "Viva la Huelga" (1968), lent openhearted support to Caesar Chavez's United Farm Workers and the long strike that followed. Davis's political imagery appealed to Papp. "The poster is for the people who can't see the show," he told Davis. His posters [for many Public Theater plays] were plastered on train platforms along the Eastern corridor and in the subways. According to producer Bernie Gersten, Davis's posters had an impact on the actors. "The poster is a mirror of the character—Sam Waterston sees his image and it informs his performance over time."

To my eyes, Davis's work said both excellence and entertainment. So, when I met him in the mid-eighties, I asked if he'd design some book jackets: for the diaries of the playwright Joe Orton, which I was editing, and for two early novels which were being reprinted. What began with a handshake is a collaboration that has lasted 20 years and

has produced 11 book jackets and more than 40 illustrations at *The New Yorker*, where I have been the senior theater critic since 1992.

Not long ago, Davis was talking on the phone to his sister, who had taken up painting. The trouble, she said, is that every time she paints a picture she's so happy with it that it's weeks before she paints another. "God, I wish I could feel that way," he said. From under a tower of work, he extricated three recent Picasso-inspired studies of his wife. "Myrna remarked that as time goes by my portraits of her are getting more affectionate." He studied his drawings for a moment. "I just go where they're leading me. I just let them go where they're going. I really enjoy that," he said.

JOHN LAHR

Excerpted from the essay for "Paul Davis: Show People,"
Edizione Nuages, 2005.

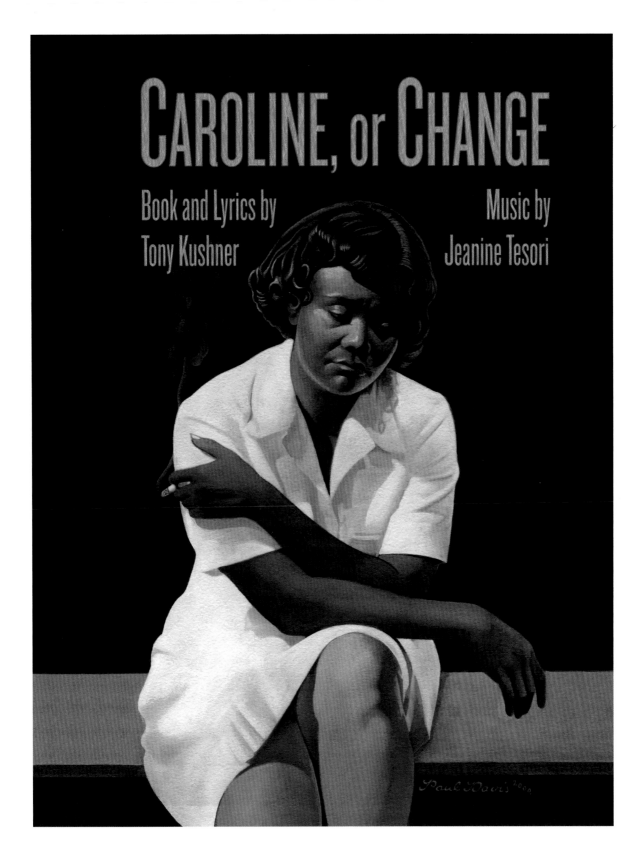

ARNOLD ROTH

[b. 1929]

Probably, the world around Arnold Roth has never seemed entirely sane to him. Throughout his work, we have his risible gloss on civilization as we know it or, more accurately, as we've tried to ignore it, an enterprise Roth seems dedicated to undermine by making us face ourselves. What he makes us see is not so much any congenital ugliness or evil, rather it is a somewhat bent reality, one that's oddly inconsistent with our more exalted aspirations. Roth's satiric vision seems more attuned to highlighting the nature of the human condition than to reforming it. He doesn't want to change us so much as he wants us to take a kind of perversely comical delight in our own idiosyncrasies as a species.

Roth has been a humorous illustrator and cartoonist all his life and, for most of that time, has freelanced, snatching a living by hustling one assignment after another in a highly competitive market, the wolf kept at bay by ingenuity and energy. And talent. And luck, Roth readily admits—even proclaims—lots of luck.

Roth had the luck to be born in 1929 on the cusp of the dawning Great Depression, so he learned the survival value of scrambling for gainful employment while growing up in Philadelphia. Roth and his older brother shared the same interests and frequented the Philadelphia Art Museum and the Philadelphia Library. They went to exhibitions and shows. Very early, Roth fell in love with jazz and learned to play the saxophone. He also drew pictures and even sold a few.

Upon graduation from high school in 1946, Roth was awarded a full scholarship to the Philadelphia Museum School of Industrial Arts, but he was expelled at the end of two years because he was always arriving late—he was playing sax in jazz bands until the wee hours of the morning and couldn't get out of bed in time for class. Roth started freelancing artwork in the summer of 1948, but until the mid-1950s, his saxophone was a more dependable source of income than his pen. For a time, Roth did all kinds of menial artistic tasks, and he worked cheap, but he was establishing a reputation for reliability and quality. In 1952, he started to get lucky: he got in on the ground floor of *TV Guide* when it went national, he married Caroline Wingfield, an artist he'd met at art school, and he met Paul

Rock Star Exhibition . The New Yorker, 1999. Medal winner at the Society of Illustrator. Photo of the artist by Anne Hall © 1996. All art courtesy of the artist.

Desmond and the rest of the Dave Brubeck Quartet, which soon led to lucrative assignments doing record album covers for that group and others. In a few years he was selling regularly enough to such magazines as *Glamour, Charm,* as well as to *TV Guide,* that he could say he was making a living as a cartoonist.

Roth had also developed a working credo that guided him through his long career. He wouldn't do preliminary sketches for approval. He wouldn't draw what they told him to draw. If they came to him with an assignment, they must have seen his work and liked it. To do that sort of work, his best work, he told his clients that he must be free to follow his maniac muse wherever it might lead him.

Roth's big breakthrough came in 1957 when he started working on *Trump, Playboy's* lavish satiric magazine, and subsequently on *Humbug,* a more penurious production, both the inventions of Harvey Kurtzman, founder of *Mad* magazine. For these short-lived but heartfelt enterprises, Roth did what he called "pure humor"—ideas executed solely for the sake of comedy and satire. He also began doing illustrations for *Playboy* and cartoons for England's *Punch* magazine, and he sold a cartoon into newspaper syndication.

Called *Poor Arnold's Almanac,* it ran for two years, beginning in May 1959. Designed as a Sunday feature, it was exactly the sort of cartooning Roth would be most adept at—and the kind he liked most to do. In each installment of the *Almanac,* the opening panel announced the topic for the day, and Roth played variations on the theme in the manner of a jazz musician, turning the subject this way and that, inspecting it from every angle and finding inconsistencies in human behavior and naked emperors everywhere he looked. The format permitted him to play with words as well as pictures, punning and making lists and reciting with sportive abandon whatever drollery he discerned in some aspect of his subject. It was vintage Roth buffoonery. And he would eventually continue in the same mode for *Punch* and *Playboy.*

In 1960, Roth went to England for a year and established himself with *Punch.* Five years later, back in the U.S., he began a 23-year gig for the magazine, doing a monthly two-page spread of cartoon reportage on the American foibles of the day, deploying the method he'd perfected in his *Almanac* for prankish flights of hilarity. In 1986, he was invited to carve his initials on the *Punch* table—a distinction afforded only about 80 persons in the magazine's 145-year history, James Thurber being the only other American.

From the mid-1960s on, Roth's work appeared regularly in most major American magazines, from *Time* and *Esquire* to *Holiday*, *New Woman*, and *Sports Illustrated*. In 1983, Roth was elected president of the National Cartoonists Society and the next year received the NCS Reuben award as cartoonist of the year. A member of the Society of Illustrators, as well as several city art directors clubs, he won many Gold and Silver Medals in the Society's annual shows. He appeared on the *Tonight Show* with Johnny Carson several times and on David Letterman's *Late Show*. He lectured at Princeton, Yale, the Philadelphia College of Art, and at numerous other art schools.

For Roth, every drawing represents an artistic challenge as well as a narrative one. The cartoonist must not only make the literal humorous point clearly—the narrative chore—but must make it in a way that is aesthetically pleasing—to the artist as much as to the reader. In meeting this challenge, Roth thinks like a jazz musician.

"I try to give myself little problems," he said. "Brubeck, years ago, was on a symposium and somebody asked him, 'Would you describe what playing jazz is?' And he said, 'It's getting yourself into and out of trouble.'

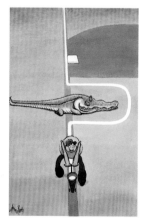

I thought that was a good way to put it. If you're not doing that, you're really hacking it, doing the same thing over and over. I always want to push it a little.

"When I illustrate," he went on, "I do a funny drawing about that subject. I won't just illustrate an occurrence in the story. I want the drawing to be comprehensible and entertaining apart from the piece. My experience is that people look at the pictures first and then they read the piece. If you're a straight illustrator, you depict an incident from the story, and the reader thinks, 'Wow—that looks exciting.' But what's the point of me drawing Joe putting his hat on the rack while Mary shoves her lover out the back door? You can do that with a photo now. Straight illustrators used to do those things. I figure my function is to entertain the person and get them into the piece. In the long run, the most important thing is the art, the actual graphic work. And I say this to people, and they say, 'Oh, no.' And I say, 'Look—none of us care what Gillray's politics were, or Rowlandson's views; you just look at those pictures. They're funny and they're great. They're beautifully done.'"

ROBERT C. HARVEY
Author, The Art of the Funnies: An Aesthetic History

ABOVE: *Street Musicians. Punch,* 1961.
OPPOSITE TOP: *Seasoned Cook: New Orleans. Esquire,* 1985.
OPPOSITE BELOW: *Spring Training. Sports Illustrated,* 1981.

MARIO COOPER

[1905–1995]

In his lifetime, Mario Cooper excelled in many roles, not the least of which was that of illustrator. His years in illustration showed his deep commitment to the magic that is design and his appreciation of research, which is so necessary to that art form. (He once built an entire cardboard staircase, complete with banister and balusters, so that he could be sure of how the light and shadows would play on it.)

Born in Mexico City in 1905, his American father brought the family to the United States to avoid the threats of the escalating Mexican revolution. But he had gotten his first taste of art from one of his teachers while in Mexico, which appears to be the germination of his artistic bent. Later, his insatiable appetite for research, old and new, set the stage for new "points of view" in his work, such as looking down from a balcony or stair landing, or leaning out a window—the introduction of a slightly new camera angle, as we would now say.

In the 1930s, when he was teaching illustration at Columbia University in New York City, some sculpture classes caught his eye. He began to try his hand at that art form and found it wonderful. So much so that Carl Sandburg called him "friend of Phidias."

However, illustration was still his love and he became known for his interpretations of stories by such authors as Agatha Christie, Clarence Buddington Kelland, Erich Maria Remarque, and many others. He even did illustrations for a story titled "The Cardinal's Mistress." The author was little known in the United States, though he was known in Rome. His name was Benito Mussolini. Unfortunately, it wasn't too long until Americans did get to know that name—but not as an author.

As time does what it relentlessly does, Mario's work with colored inks led to experiments with watercolors and how they play on various types of paper. Photography continued to make serious inroads into what had once been the exclusive markets of the illustrator. Slowly, he was drawn into fine art, the fine art of pure watercolor, which he watched grow into a force-field of its own. No longer was watercolor trapped by the definition of "Ladies' Sunday Painting Recreational Activity."

Still, illustration prevailed in his career and he taught the subject at Pratt Institute at a time when the world was recovering from the devastation of World War II. In the war's aftermath, the United States Air Force was born, becoming a separate branch of the Armed Services. During the Civil War, the Army and Navy had learned the value of collecting art regarding their own services. The Air Force had now come of age and in 1950 instituted the U.S. Air Force Art Program to document the ongoing history of military aviation and aeronautics.

Air Force Major Robert Bales, as well as being an ace fighter pilot, was also an artist and knew of the Society of Illustrators. In 1953, the Air Force made a pact with the Society: In exchange for transportation and a per diem, the illustrators would donate their artwork to the Air Force. In September of 1954, Mario Cooper was assigned a plane with crew of seven, as well as a courtesy rank of Brigadier General. Over the years he made visits to Asia, Europe, Africa, and Alaska, accompanied by other artist members of the Society.

NASA also enlisted aid from the Society for a fantastic collection of art about America's space program, including the moon landing, exploration, etc. One of the many paintings Mario donated is a painting of a missile launch, which he had done from sketches and photos taken at Cape Canaveral, Florida. A majority of his work

ABOVE: *Beggars All*. For a story by Catherine Newlin Burt for *Woman's Home Companion*, 1932. Colored ink. OPPOSITE: *Merchant of Valor*. Saint Francis of Assissi for a story by Clarence Budington Kelland in *Collier's Weekly*, 1947. Colored Ink. Portrait by Floyd Davis. From the *Society of Illustrators Bulletin*, c. 1950s. All art courtesy of the Museum of American Illustration at the Society of Illustrators.

remains in the Pentagon and at the Smithsonian Institution in Washington, D.C.

While putting together these memories of Mario, whom I married in 1964, I thought it might not be amiss to add a memory of my own—one that has been popping into my head as I write.

I recall a winter day in Chicago. The year was 1932. My sister Gretchen, who was 17, and I, a rambunctious ten, were lounging on the bed. She had turned on the overhead and I didn't like its stark light. But she needed it to look at her magazines. She was "ooh-ing and ah-ing" over the stories and the illustrations that accompanied them. This was years ago and you may not remember those times when we had no television. Magazines like *Women's Home Companion, Ladies' Home Journal, McCall's,* and *Collier's* were the amusements for women.

Gretchen tried to get me interested but I was not. Being Tarzan was my thing, running around with a rubber knife in my belt. That was more like it. She insisted on showing me an illustration that had a monkey on a woman's shoulder. (After all, there are monkeys in the jungle, but usually not on a gal's shoulder. Any Tarzan knows that!)

That is about all I remember of the incident. I do not recall looking at magazines ever again with my sister, but I do know that I was ten, which made this memory all the more intriguing. You see, Mario illustrated a story for *Collier's* entitled "The Old Rake." It has a woman going up a stairway with a monkey on her shoulder. A man is below looking up at them. I have the original illustration in my collection and guess what? It was first published in 1932, when I was ten.

So, I may have "met" Mario thirty-two years before I married him.

DALE MEYERS COOPER

CLOCKWISE FROM TOP: *Almost a Gypsy.* For a story by Conrad Bercovici in *American Magazine,* 1934. Colored ink; *Stick Up.* For *Collier's,* 1933. Wash; *Examining a Portrait.* For a story by Agatha Christie in *Collier's Weekly,* 1934. Colored ink.

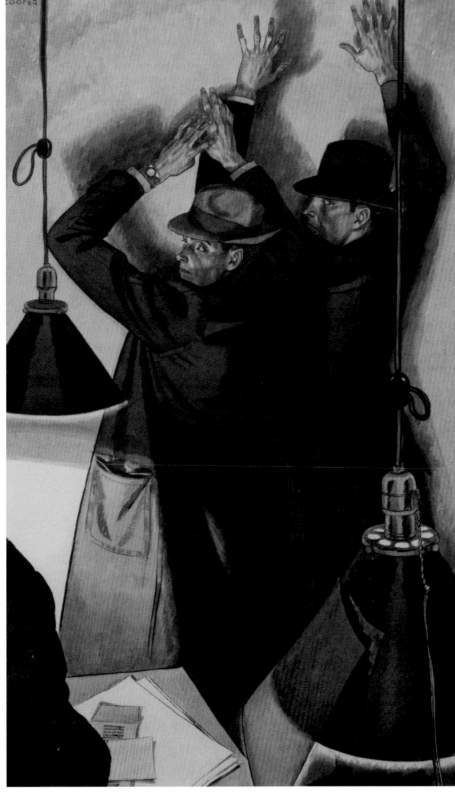

LAURENCE FELLOWS

[1885–1964]

From the Gay Nineties up through the 1920s, American humor magazines played a greater social role than is generally appreciated. Their candor in recording the current events in a satirical weekly or monthly forum presented the contemporary American attitudes, prejudices, and mores in the guise of humor that was not found in the more sober mainstream periodicals. Publications such as *Truth, Life, Puck, Leslie's,* and *Judge* showcased the talents of such major illustrators as Charles Dana Gibson, James Montgomery Flagg, Orson Lowell, T.S. Sullivant, Peter Newell, Art Young, and many others who mirrored the country's foibles in their enthusiastic ridicule.

Joining the group in the early teens was an ultra sophisticated young artist named Laurence Fellows. A native of Pennsylvania, Fellows had received his training at the Philadelphia Academy of Art, with several follow-up years studying in England and in France at the Academie Julien under J.P. Laurens.

Upon his return to the United States, Fellows' fresh point of view, particularly reflecting a French/*Vogue* influence, found him a ready audience. His style was distinguished by a thin outline, flat tonality or color, with the emphasis on shapes rather than details. Just as quickly, however, he acquired many imitators. Before John Held, Jr., for instance, had invented his "flapper," he was clearly adapting much from Fellows' mannered drawing style into his own submitted gags. Other new converts were Hal Burroughs, Bertram Hartman, and Ralph Barton, who would each run with it in their own way. Fellows particularly liked to play with off-balanced compositions, even in the more conservative arena of illustration for advertising.

One of his early commercial clients was Kelly-Springfield Tires, which gave him the opportunity to combine his elegant draftsmanship with the clever, humorous copy depreciating the competition, thus often violating the rule against "negative" advertising. But Fellows' drawing and the copy had an edge of good humor that attracted a national following and the successful campaign lasted for many years.

In the thirties, Fellows gradually shifted his emphasis to fashion art, including both men and women, finding clients in *Vanity Fair, Vogue, Cosmopolitan, The American Magazine,* and *McClure's.* He also became a regular contributor to *Apparel Arts* magazine.

With only a limited number of men's fashion artists available, Fellows was most in demand for the male-focused subjects, particularly by the newly launched *Esquire* magazine in the thirties, where he was regularly featured in full-color spreads for many years.

Although Fellows considered himself a commercial illustrator, he was also a painter who exhibited periodically, later concentrating on abstractions.

In reviewing his entire career, however, it is his early work, when he found a fresh viewpoint in a sophisticated spoof of the social upper crust, that makes us admire his audacity and leaves us with a smile of appreciation.

WALT REED
Illustration House

ABOVE: *Hyde Park, London.* Hon. Freddy—"Haven't the foggiest idea, old chap—Ridley (waxing warm)"Kelly-Springfields, Sir—American, nothing to touch 'em—never blow or skid—a bit of orl right, sir, you ask me!" Ad in *Vanity Fair,* 1923. OPPOSITE: Illustration for Kelly-Springfield tires, January 17, 1920. Courtesy of Illustration House.

ABOVE AND LEFT: Both illustrations for stories by J.A. Waldron in *Caricature—The Wit & Humor of a Nation in Picture, Song & Story, Illustrated by America's Greatest Artists.* Published by Leslie-Judge Company, circa 1917–1918. Courtesy of Illustration House.

TOP: *Dispatch Riders on Duty in France.* From "The End of Rivalry" by J.A. Waldron. *Judge,* 1917. Gouache. Courtesy of the Museum of American Illustration at the Society of Illustrators; ABOVE: *A Very Narrow Escape.* For the story by J.A. Waldron in *Caricature—The Wit & Humor of a Nation in Picture, Song & Story, Illustrated by America's Greatest Artists.* Published by Leslie-Judge Company, circa 1917–1918. Courtesy of Illustration House; LEFT: *Fashion Is Always On the Come and Go. Esquire,* November 1936. Courtesy of Illustration House.

HERBERT MORTON STOOPS

[1888 – 1948]

The son of a Mormon preacher and his Ohioan wife, Herbert Morton Stoops was born in 1888 in Logan City, Utah, about 70 miles south of Yellowstone National Park. At some point in Herbert's childhood the Stoops family moved to a ranch in Idaho—then a wild, sparsely populated land in the infancy of its statehood, and home to some of the most spectacular and rugged scenery in the United States. In those days, Native American tribes such as the Bannock, Shoshone, Kootenai, and Nez Percé still roamed Idaho's plains and mountains, and camped on the shores of its many rivers and lakes. Young Stoops grew up during the twilight of the vanishing Old West, amidst ranchers, miners, cowboys and Indians—larger-than-life characters who would later people many of his illustrations and paintings. The vast open sky was his earliest canvas, and his artist's eye studied the proportions of every creature under it: oxen, cattle, mules, and above all, horses—wild or tame, standing still or galloping hell for leather, it didn't matter; throughout his career Stoops was uniquely able to imbue his two-dimensional horses with a spirit of snorting, straining, three-dimensional life.

Encouraged, perhaps, by his clergyman father, young Herbert went on to pursue a higher education, attending Utah State College, where he graduated in 1905. In college he took his first formal art classes. This early training—added to his innate ability and the vibrant images he'd been stockpiling throughout his youth—appears to have stood him in good stead, because by 1910 Herbert Morton Stoops had already gained employment as a staff artist for the *San Francisco Chronicle*, and later, for the *San Francisco Examiner*.

In 1914, Stoops moved to Chicago, where he took classes at the Art Institute while working as a staff artist for the *Chicago Tribune*. He was beginning to make a name for himself as a newspaper illustrator, and was also starting to do black-and-white drawings, page decorations, and story headings for *Blue Book*, the prestigious literary pulp magazine with which he would be identified for the rest of his life. Drawings were also published and color covers made for long defunct and forgotten magazines such as *Illustrated World* and others.

But by this time the world was at war, so the budding artist enlisted in the Army, serving in France as First Lieutenant in the Sixth Field Artillery of the First Division. While overseas, Stoops sent drawings from his

sketchbook back to the home front, captivating the American public with his firsthand pictorial accounts of soldiers and battle. A compilation of his wartime sketches, *Inked Memories of 1918*, was published in 1924.

After the war, Stoops moved to New York City and married Elise Borough. Under the tutelage of famed artist Harvey Dunn, Stoops applied all his early experiences to canvas and paper and perfected his craft. No longer just a promising talent, he was becoming one of the most sought-after illustrators of his day. By the early '20s, large oils by Herbert Morton Stoops were being featured in *Cosmopolitan* and *Good Housekeeping* alongside the works of Dean Cornwell, N.C. Wyeth, and other illustration giants. The oils were most often painted in color but were reproduced as black-and-whites with an occasional duotone two-color effect. Stoops's work appeared in interior stories and covers for all the major magazines of the era, including *Collier's*, *Liberty*, and *McCall's*. During this time he also began painting covers for *The American Legion Magazine*, a publication for which he would work constantly in the years to come.

Stoops's talent proved as vast and sprawling as the western landscape from which he hailed. While many of his contemporaries became known for a signature style, Herbert Morton Stoops was a master of all media and genres. From charcoal and pencil drawing to pen-and-ink with splashes of thin wash, from tempura and watercolor to heavyweight oils, he did it all and he did it well. Such proficiency and versatility made him the perfect illustrator for the powerful and dramatic stories that ran in pulp publications. Stoops had been a contributing artist to the pages of *Blue Book* previous to World War I, but he'd grown as an artist since then, and editor Donald Kendicott soon took notice and assigned him a cover.

Stoops's first *Blue Book* cover featured a new character in pulpdom—*Kioga Hawk*, a Tarzan-like figure, adopted by the ancestors of Native Americans in the Wild West of the Ice Age. The W.H. Chester

FACING PAGE: *Zeppelin Watch at Dover. American Legion Magazine*, 1916. Oil on canvas. Courtesy of the Museum of American Illustration at the Society of Illustrators. Photograph of the artist courtesy of Colonel Charles Waterhouse.

story, brought to bold, adventurous life with his exciting illustrations, soon became a favorite of readers. Interestingly enough, while the cover art was credited to Herbert Morton Stoops, the beautiful black-and-white illustrations inside the publication were credited to Jeremy Cannon—one of two pseudonyms Stoops would use frequently throughout his career. He also illustrated many serials and articles in charcoal pencil under the assumed name Raymond Sisley—the names Sisley and Cannon most likely referring back to the artist's artillery experiences during the First World War.

Editor Kendicott knew great illustration when he saw it, and in 1935 he commissioned Herbert Morton Stoops to paint all of *Blue Book*'s monthly covers and gave him first pick of interior stories to illustrate. Kendicott had the reputation of being a perceptive, kindly, and intelligent man—someone who maintained a close familial relationship with his stable of writers and artists. Stoops had a talent that was bigger than any one medium and any one name. Their creative collaboration would last until the artist's death in 1948.

In 1940 Stoops received the Isidor Medal from the National Academy for his work, *Anno Domini*, which depicted the ravages of war on refugees. During World War II he did several posters for the office of War Information. One that he painted right after V-E Day garnered particular praise and demand. Designed to combat victory let-down on the home front, it showed an American prisoner of war behind barbed wire, grimly staring past his Japanese guard, and featured the inscription: "The War's Not Over 'Til Our Last Man Is Free."

A member of the Salmagundi Club, the Society of Illustrators, and the American Artists' Professional League, Stoops had a strong influence on an emerging generation of artists, including pulp illustrators A.L. Ross and H.W. Scott. A rising star in Harvey Dunn's illustration

classroom, Steven R. Kidd recalled being stopped in his tracks during a visit to Mr. Stoops's studio. "You look like your draw from the wrists down," Stoops said, in critiquing one of Kidd's line drawings. He went on to add that even the great Howard Pyle in his early years sometimes looked like he was drawing with his feet—although Pyle's impeccable design and composition managed to overpower his stilted drawing. The comment made a lasting impression on Kidd.

Stoops was working on a series of monthly covers for *Blue Book* based on the history of each of the then-48 states when, on May 19, 1948, after a prolonged period of failing health and several weeks of illness, he died at his art studio residence on Barrow Street in Greenwich Village, New York City. He was only 60 years old but he had left a legacy of thousands of unforgettable images that had engaged, excited, and delighted the American public.

In retrospect, Stoops's immense success in the pulps and magazines may have been a double-edged sword. The very fact that he drew so freely, and could produce pictures in any medium, presented a dilemma: he was inundated with pulp assignments, often to the detriment of the large and important oil paintings that would have secured his place in the forefront of the Western art genre, along with painters such as W.H.D. Koerner, Harvey Dunn, Harold Von Schmidt, and Benton and Matt Clark. That being said, over the span of nearly four decades Herbert Morton Stoops was one of the few illustrators who had the best of all worlds, creating art for major magazines and pulps, newspapers, books, advertising, and galleries, and approaching each and every assignment with the same degree of artistic skill, professionalism, and passion.

Colonel Charles Waterhouse
Colonel Waterhouse Museum

ABOVE: *Lover's Farewell*. Oil on canvas. Courtesy of the Museum of American Illustration at the Society of Illustrators. LEFT: *Centralization*. For the story "Centralization" in *Pictorial Review*, August 11, 1923. Courtesy of the Museum of American Illustration at the Society of Illustrators. FACING PAGE: Work by Herbert Morton Stoops signed Raymond Sisely for a series of works for *American Legion Magazine* in the early 1920s. Courtesy of Colonel Charles Waterhouse.

1958 Norman Rockwell
1959 Dean Cornwell
     Harold Von Schmidt
1960 Fred Cooper
1961 Floyd Davis
1962 Edward Wilson
1963 Walter Biggs
1964 Arthur William Brown
1965 Al Parker
1966 Al Dorne
1967 Robert Fawcett
1968 Peter Helck
1969 Austin Briggs
1970 Rube Goldberg
1971 Stevan Dohanos
1972 Ray Prohaska
1973 Jon Whitcomb
1974 Tom Lovell
     Charles Dana Gibson*
     N.C. Wyeth*
1975 Bernie Fuchs
     Maxfield Parrish*
     Howard Pyle*
1976 John Falter
     Winslow Homer*
     Harvey Dunn*
1977 Robert Peak
     Wallace Morgan*
     J.C. Leyendecker*
1978 Coby Whitmore
     Norman Price*
     Frederic Remington*
1979 Ben Stahl
     Edwin Austin Abbey*
     Lorraine Fox*
1980 Saul Tepper
     Howard Chandler Christy*
     James Montgomery Flagg*

1981 Stan Galli
     Frederic R. Gruger*
     John Gannam*
1982 John Clymer
     Henry P. Raleigh*
     Eric (Carl Erickson)*
1983 Mark English
     Noel Sickles*
     Franklin Booth*
1984 Neysa Moran McMein*
     John LaGatta*
     James Williamson*
1985 Robert Weaver
     Charles Marion Russell*
     Arthur Burdett Frost*
1986 Al Hirschfeld
     Rockwell Kent*
1987 Maurice Sendak
     Haddon Sundblom*
1988 Robert T. McCall
     René Bouché*
     Pruett Carter*
1989 Erté
     John Held Jr.*
     Arthur Ignatius Keller*
1990 Burt Silverman
     Robert Riggs*
     Morton Roberts*
1991 Donald Teague
     Jessie Willcox Smith*
     William A. Smith*

1992 Joe Bowler
     Edwin A. Georgi*
     Dorothy Hood*
1993 Robert McGinnis
     Thomas Nast*
     Coles Phillips*
1994 Harry Anderson
     Elizabeth Shippen Green*
     Ben Shahn*
1995 James Avati
     McClelland Barclay*
     Joseph Clement Coll*
     Frank E. Schoonover*
1996 Herb Tauss
     Anton Otto Fischer*
     Winsor McCay*
     Violet Oakley*
     Mead Schaeffer*
1997 Diane and Leo Dillon
     Frank McCarthy
     Chesley Bonestell*
     Joe DeMers*
     Maynard Dixon*
     Harrison Fisher*
1998 Robert M. Cunningham
     Frank Frazetta
     Boris Artzybasheff*
     Kerr Eby*
     Edward Penfield*
     Martha Sawyers*
1999 Mitchell Hooks
     Stanley Meltzoff
     Andrew Loomis*
     Antonio Lopez*
     Thomas Moran*
     Rose O'Neill*
     Adolph Treidler*

2000 James Bama
     Alice and Martin* Provensen
     Nell Brinkley*
     Charles Livingston Bull*
     David Stone Martin*
     J. Allen St. John*
2001 Howard Brodie
     Franklin McMahon
     John James Audubon*
     William H. Bradley*
     Felix Octavius Carr Darley*
     Charles R. Knight*
2002 Milton Glaser
     Daniel Schwartz
     Elmer Simms Campbell*
     Jean Leon Huens*
2003 Elaine Duillo
     David Levine
     Bill Mauldin*
     Jack Potter*
2004 John Berkey
     Robert Andrew Parker
     John Groth*
     Saul Steinberg*
2005 Jack Davis
     Brad Holland
     Albert Beck Wenzell*
     Herbert Paus*

2006 Keith Ferris
    Alvin J. Pimsler
    Jack Unruh
    Gilbert Bundy*
    Bradshaw Crandall*
    Hal Foster*
    Frank H. Netter, M.D.*
2007 David Grove
    Gary Kelley
    Edward Windsor Kemble*
    Russell Patterson*
    George Stavrinos*
2008 Kinuko Y. Craft
    Naiad Einsel
    Walter Einsel*
    Benton Clark*
    Matt Clark*
2009 Paul Davis
    Arnold Roth
    Mario Cooper*
    Laurence Fellows*
    Herbert Morton Stoops*

HALL OF FAME COMMITTEE 2009

Chairman
    Murray Tinkelman

Chairman Emeritus
    Willis Pyle

Former Presidents
    Richard Berenson
    Vincent Di Fate
    Diane Dillon
    Judy Francis Zankel
    Al Lorenz
    Charles McVicker
    Wendell Minor
    Howard Munce
    Alvin J. Pimsler
    Shannon Stirnweis
    Steven Stroud
    John Witt

*Presented posthumously

2009 HAMILTON KING AWARD
AND
RICHARD GANGEL ART DIRECTOR AWARD

The Hamilton King Award, created by Mrs. Hamilton King in memory of her husband through a bequest, is presented annually for the best illustration of the year by a member of the Society. The selection is made by former recipients of this award and may be won only once.

The Richard Gangel Art Director Award was established in 2005 to honor art directors currently working in the field who have supported and advanced the art of illustration. This award is named in honor of Richard Gangel (1918 – 2002), the influential art director at *Sports Illustrated* from 1960 to 1981, whose collaboration with illustrators during that period was exceptional.

Tim O'Brien

[b. 1964]

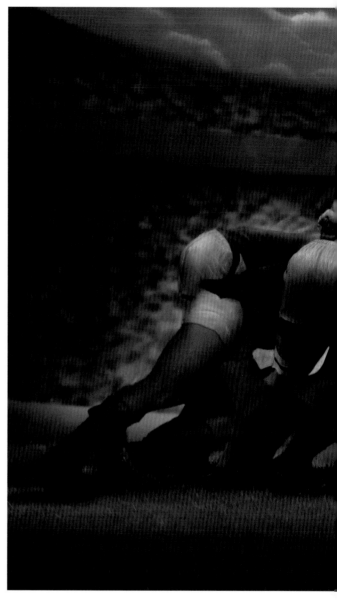

It was on the pages of the Society of Illustrators annuals that I first 'met' Tim O'Brien. I can't remember which image struck me first, but we've all seen them: the locomotive roaring across the ocean, the crazed young man doused in gasoline, the tiny elephant balanced on the tips of a human's fingers. Tim's meticulous skills and surprising concepts were impressive and slightly intimidating. But, as a young designer in children's publishing poring over those annuals, I knew I wanted to work with this artist, and I knew I wanted to meet the man who created this work.

I commissioned Tim for the first time in 1988. It was a teen horror cover, something like a strangled teddy bear with a bloody dagger. This was not the genre Tim was meant for—he was doing jobs for

Playboy and other adult publishing clients within his first year out of school. But lifeless teddy bears and surprised kids were the sorts of assignments I was given back then. And I needed the excuse to work with Tim.

I worked with Tim for at least a year before we finally met in 1989 at a business lunch. I was surprised to discover how young Tim was. In fact, we had graduated from art school the same year. His art seemed so much more *experienced*. At that first meeting, we sat next to each other, talking intently for two hours. We were both intrigued.

I learned quite a bit about Tim during that conversation. I learned of his father's death when he was only nine years old, about his dedication to boxing, and about the care he gave three children in his rough Philadelphia neighborhood. He had taken in these fatherless children for two months, bought them clothes, and taken them to the dentist. He clearly had a generous spirit. I was smitten.

After a handful of phone calls over a few months, I convinced Tim to go on a date with me—more like a weekend away. That weekend solidified our relationship, working and otherwise. Eight months later he moved to Brooklyn and in with me.

Now, I was living with this impressive artist, and was there to see his amazing concepts go from napkin, to sketchbook, to board. He was no

longer so intimidating, and we fed off each other's roles in the business.

Our career trajectories moved on similar, upward paths. Through Tim I met a community of artists, and my role as an art director matured and grew. I continued to commission Tim for such projects as the Royal Diaries portrait series, and numerous literary hard covers. While Tim continued to work with his regular clients, he was suddenly in demand with important news periodicals as well. *Time* began to commission him regularly, as did *Business Week* and *Der Spiegel*. Then our personal trajectories joined even more completely. We got married.

Tim has always impressed me with his ability to juggle his illustration jobs, while making time to give to others. He was chairman of the Society of Illustrators Student Scholarship Competition for ten years, taught illustration at University of the Arts, and gave painting

tips to his illustrator friends when they asked. I often wondered how he could give his trade secrets. Tim also taught boxing at the local YMCA four nights a week—for free! He shares his talent and his skills so generously.

Tim's work has been included in every SI annual for the last 22 years. And he has won a few medals. But one award he only *dreamed* of receiving was the Hamilton King. *I* knew he deserved one, but if he did too, he never let on.

When he heard the announcement of his selection at the Editorial and Book opening of Illustrators 51, he was, to use an English term *very*

appropriate for a boxer, *gobsmacked*. As he walked up to the podium to speak, many of his friends and colleagues patted him on the back, saying that it was "long overdue," and "about time."

To be chosen for the Hamilton King award by this outstanding group of previous winners, is, I know, a great thrill for Tim. And although it is given in acknowledgment for one piece of art in particular, we know it comes to him as recognition, too, of his extensive body of work, and his great but humble contribution to the illustration profession. I can't think of a more deserving artist. And, as one of his many art directors, *and* as his wife, I can say: *Well, of course!*

Congratulations, Timmy.

ELIZABETH PARISI
Executive Art Director, Trade Hard covers, Scholastic Inc.

Scrum, for art director Kevin O'Shea at Rothco Advertising. Oil on board. Portrait by Cassius O'Brien.

GAIL ANDERSON

Gail Anderson embodies three virtues: inspiring art director, inspired designer, and inspirational teacher. Despite being deceptively low key, she does everything with intense passion. Her extreme devotion to craft (she often frets for ages over the minutest typographic detail) combined with an unceasing, though always natural, pursuit of whimsy distinguishes her brand of quirkiness from the larger pack of knee-jerk quirks. While some might choose to call her method retro, the work defies stylistic pigeon-holing. She revels in making typography from old and new forms, which is neither modernist nor post-modernist, but rather spot-on contemporaneous.

Working with Fred Woodward at *Rolling Stone* was a hand-in-glove experience. They knew each other about as well as two people could. "Music always set the tone and he was into low lighting, so the design room felt sort of cozy," Anderson recalls. "And he'd just howl with glee when we 'got it' and it was a winner. He could really get you jazzed about the process, even when it was difficult." Anderson's own typographic proclivities were ultimately well suited to *Rolling Stone*, where she designed what might best be called "theatrical typography."

Anderson has a special gift for assigning illustration and has been a stalwart advocate of illustrators. "With her keen eye for fresh talent, she nurtured a whole generation of illustrators," says Woodward, "while staying loyal to the greats as well."

The most difficult time in her career came in 2002, after her move to SpotCo, when negotiating the transition from editorial design to advertising. "You approach each project searching for a dozen great ideas, not just one or two," Anderson explains of how her work competes for the attention (and dollars) of theatergoers.

Typographically, Anderson is always looking for that little visual wink or tiny gesture of extra care. "I'm all about the wood type bits and pieces. I love making those crunchy little objects into other things, like faces,"

she says. A fancy border and detailed extras are always part of her repertoire. "I'd ask the designers I work with to put them on everything, if I could," Anderson says. "Of course, it's not always appropriate and sometimes the more straightforward approach is more confident or what's called for. But any little bit of extra attention is always welcomed, and I just hope that the client won't ask for it to be removed."

More often than not, however, Anderson admits that even in her theater posters the ornamentation is peeled off little by little. "I guess there's concern that consumers will get mesmerized or confused by the detailing and forget to buy tickets. But if we've done our job properly, the doo-dads become part of the package, and not something getting in the way that needs to be reduced or cut out."

For its human dimension, the art for *The Good Body*, a play about women and body image by *The Vagina Monologues* author, Eve Ensler, struck just the right chord with its Isabelle Dervaux line drawing and the ice cream scoop breasts. But Anderson may be best known for the *Avenue Q* subway/puppet fur logo, a delightfully witty image that became an indelible brand for the play. "I'm definitely wittier on paper than in real life," she laments, "I think I approach the work looking for a little wink where I can, because deep down, I hope people associate clever with smart. Or maybe in the end, if I think of it as disposable, I'm less likely to fear experimenting a little."

For much of her career Anderson has been the quintessential collaborator because, as she notes, "it's more fun to work with other designers and art directors; I really enjoy the back and forth." These days, though, she likes designing alone, "in *my* office, with *my* music on." She adds, "Most high-octane, solo designing has to be done at night. I'm trying to change my ways before I look up and I'm 50." Heaven forbid.

STEVEN HELLER
Co-chair MFA Designer as Author, School of Visual Arts

Portrait by Paul Davis.

HAMILTON KING AWARD

[1965–2009]

1965 Paul Calle	1974 Fred Otnes	1984 Braldt Bralds	1991 Brad Holland	2000 Mark Summers
1966 Bernie Fuchs	1975 Carol Anthony	1985 Attila Hejja	1992 Gary Kelley	2001 James Bennett
1967 Mark English	1976 Judith Jampel	1986 Doug Johnson	1993 Jerry Pinkney	2002 Peter de Sève
1968 Robert Peak	1977 Leo & Diane Dillon	1987 Kinuko Y. Craft	1994 John Collier	2003 Anita Kunz
1969 Alan E. Cober	1978 Daniel Schwartz	1988 James McMullan	1995 C.F. Payne	2004 Michael Deas
1970 Ray Ameijide	1979 William Teason	1989 Guy Billout	1996 Etienne Delessert	2005 Steve Brodner
1971 Miriam Schottland	1980 Wilson McLean	1990 Edward Sorel	1997 Marshall Arisman	2006 John Thompson
1972 Charles Santore	1981 Gerald McConnell		1998 Jack Unruh	2007 Ted Lewin
1973 Dave Blossom	1982 Robert Heindel		1999 Gregory Manchess	2008 Donato Giancola
	1983 Robert M. Cunningham			2009 Tim O'Brien

RICHARD GANGEL ART DIRECTOR AWARD

[2005-2009]

2005 Steven Heller

2006 Fred Woodward

2007 Rita Marshall

2008 Patrick J.B. Flynn

2009 Gail Anderson

Editorial

N. ASCENCIOS
ILLUSTRATOR

Natalie Ascencios's work first appeared in *The New Yorker*, *The New York Times Book Review*, *Rolling Stone*, *Time*, as well as other publications. Natalie's paintings can also be seen in the various competitive annuals of the Society of Illustrators, *American Illustration*, *Communication Arts* and the *Print* annuals. The Society of Illustrators has awarded her one Gold Medal and two Silver Medals. She also received first place in puppetry in the Henson design competition. She has taught drawing at the School of Visual Arts graduate and undergraduate schools and has given talks on painting, drawing, and memory, and has had exhibitions throughout the country and abroad. The artist lives in Brooklyn, where she keeps a studio.

SERGE BLOCH
ILLUSTRATOR

Born in Colmar (Alsace), France, in 1956, Serge Bloch studied at the School of Decorative Arts in Strasbourg. An illustrator and author of children's books, Serge works for many publications, including *The Washington Post*, *Wall*, *The Chicago Tribune*, *The New York Times*, *Time*, *New York*, *The Boston Globe*, *GQ*, *The Los Angeles Times*, *Ecologist Magazine* in England, and in France: *Liberation*, *Psychologies*, and *La Vie*. The art director for a French publisher of children's magazines and books, he created Samsam, a character who is a small superhero, for a series of comic books. An animated TV series with Samsam is broadcast in Europe. His last book published in the U.S., *The Enemy*, which got the support of Amnesty International, is dear to his heart.

JOSH COCHRAN
ILLUSTRATOR

Josh Cochran's drawings are commissioned by a variety of clients in broadcast, book and magazine publishing, and advertising. He has received awards from several publications and organizations, including *Print*'s New Visual Artists 2009, ADC Young Guns 6, the Society of Illustrators, *American Illustration*, *3x3*, and was recently featured on the cover of *Communication Arts*. Josh lives in Brooklyn with his wife Jenny and small dog Porkchop, and in his spare time enjoys working on silkscreen prints.

FERNANDA COHEN
ILLUSTRATOR

Fernanda Cohen is from Buenos Aires and has been based in New York City since 2000. She graduated from the School of Visual Arts, where she's now a faculty member. She has received over 60 awards worldwide, including a Silver Medal from the Society of Illustrators in New York, Gold and Silver Medals from the Society of Illustrators of LA, first prize from *Creative Review* (UK), first and second place from Altpick, *Communication Arts*, *3x3*, *American Illustration*, *Lüzer's Archive*, *HOW*, *STEP Inside Design*, and *Graphis*. Clients include *The New Yorker*, *The New York Times Magazine*, Target, MTV, Sony, *Time*, Soho House Hotels, W Hotels, DDB, BBDO, and Scholastic. Fernanda coordinates and moderates lectures at the Society of Illustrators in New York and is currently the vice president of the board of directors of ICON6.

THOMAS FUCHS
ILLUSTRATOR

Thomas Fuchs was born and raised in Germany. After finishing his studies at the Academy of Fine Arts Stuttgart with an MFA in Illustration, he moved to New York City in November 1997. Since then he has worked for most publications in the U.S. and many abroad, including *The New York Times*, *The New Yorker*, *Time*, *Rolling Stone*, *GQ*, and *Esquire*, to name a few. His work has received awards from The Society of Illustrators (Gold Medal), *American Illustration*, *Communication Arts*, *Print*, SPD, The Art Directors Club, *3x3* and The Society for News Designers (Silver Medal). He currently lives and works in New York City.

JILLIAN TAMAKI
ILLUSTRATOR

Jillian Tamaki grew up in the Canadian prairies but now lives in Brooklyn, New York. She has been illustrating since 2003, when she graduated from the Alberta College of Art and Design with a Bachelor of Design. Her clients include *The New York Times*, *The New Yorker*, *The Washington Post*, *Esquire*, *SPIN*, Penguin Canada, and the Canadian Broadcasting Company. Awards include Gold Medals from the Society of Illustrators and the Society of Publication Designers. In 2006 Conundrum Press (Montreal) released *Gilded Lilies*, a small book of her mini-comics and drawings. Jillian began teaching in the illustration department at Parsons School of Design in Fall 2007.

CATHLEEN TOELKE
ILLUSTRATOR

Based near Rhinebeck, NY, Cathleen Toelke began working as a full-time artist in 1980. Her work has regularly received awards from major illustration annuals, and she has been profiled in *Communication Arts*, *Print*, and *American Artist/ Watercolor* magazines. She is known for her editorial paintings on book covers, especially many exotic, emotionally charged ones for celebrated authors such as Gabriel Garcia Marquez, Oscar Hiluelos, and Laura Esquivel. A favorite project is a mural-sized oil painting for the lobby of the Millennium Hotels and Resorts' Premier Hotel, Times Square. Clients include the Millennium Hotels, Simon & Schuster, Random House, *GQ*, HarperCollins, Levi's, and New York University. Cathleen has been a guest speaker at the Society of Illustrators, Rhode Island School of Design, Syracuse University, AIGA, Savanna College of Art and Design, Parsons, Illustration Conference, Norman Rockwell Museum, Rochester Institute of Technology, and The New School.

JASON TREAT
ART DIRECTOR,
THE ATLANTIC

Jason Treat has been the art director for *The Atlantic* since December 2005. He previously served as the art director for Atlantic Media Company's creative services, designing in-house creative for *The Atlantic*, *National Journal*, *Government Executive*, *The Hotline*, and other publications.

Networker *Cover*
I don't remember how many different approaches we tried with art director Caren Rosenblatt to convey the idea of "possible insecure voting machines." When we thought we had it, the editor did not. I cannot remember how we got to the version that finally made it to the cover. But what I do remember is that what could have been a true nightmare, ended up being a great experience, thanks to Caren.

GOLD MEDAL WINNER
SAM WEBER

Real World
For a book review of Natsuo Kirino's *Real World*, this picture was inspired by a small sculpture of four intertwined fox heads I found in a book of traditional Japanese art. I'm still not entirely sure what this image is about, although it seems strangely fitting for this story about identity, anxiety, and the relationship between four Japanese high school girls and a boy who beats his own mother to death.

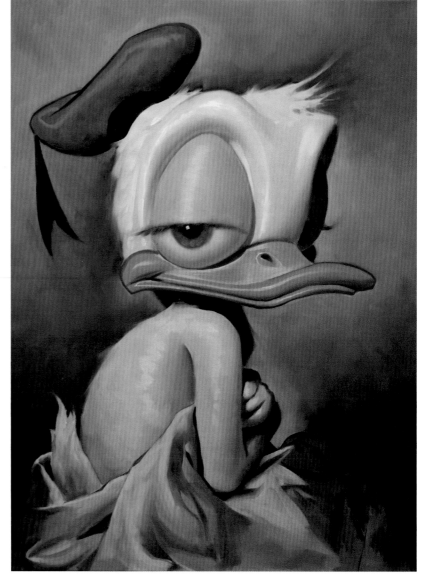

Miley Duck

This piece constituted *Vanity Fair's* response to the horrified reaction at Disney over the controversial Miley Cyrus cover by Annie Leibovitz. The only technical challenge was that I had to search for hours for just the right eggs to paint for the eyes. It was a bit surreal to see someone at the next table in a cafe in the South of France turn to the very page with my illustration on it; it's not every day an illustrator is asked for his signature. *Miley Duck* led to an offer to do a whole show of oversized Donald Ducks in erotic poses in a Moscow gallery. I was tempted, but decided for the time being to concentrate on carburetors.

Death With Interruptions
This illustration was for *The New York Times Book Review*, for the book *Death With Interruptions* written by the Nobel Prize winner Jose Saramago. In short, the story is about Death, who stops doing her job one New Year's Day. Happiness quickly turns into panic because severe problems arise when people stop passing away. It threatens to bankrupt the government's pension fund, funeral and retirement homes start closing, and so forth. Death starts doing her job again when she meets a soul as lonely as she is—a cellist who fills her dry heart with love. Because of the cello's color and shape, I thought it could represent Death's heart. There is a strong contrast between the light grey bones, black gown, and the colored cellist in Death's chest.

DANIEL ADEL

Elliot Spitzer

It's always a thrill to be called upon to recreate someone *in flagrante delicto*. Particularly when it involves a moral crusader like Spitzer. I'm not generally big on Schadenfreude, but I made a rare exception for the debauched governor. When it's so richly deserved it is very entertaining to watch the mighty take a tumble. Art director David Harris made sure I included the ultimate bizarre detail of this sordid affair: the black socks which Spitzer always kept on—throughout.

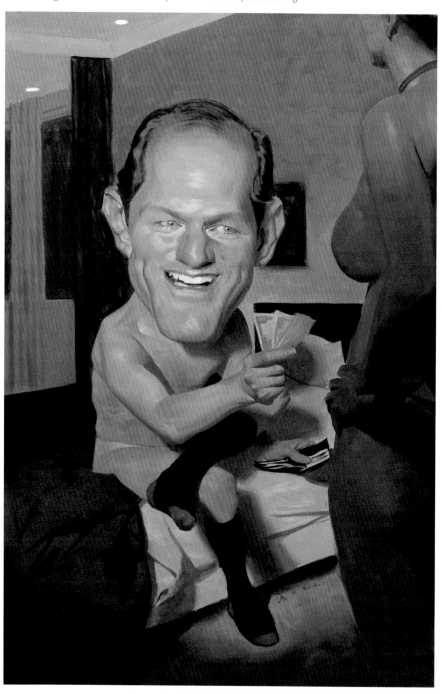

ISTVAN BANYAI
Post-Birthday World

ANA BENAROYA

Tattooman

This piece was created for the "Bells & Whistles" section of *Plansponsor* magazine. When art director SooJin Buzelli explained the assignment to me, it was pretty much an open interpretation of the phrase itself. In my mind, "bells & whistles" meant "over the top and extravagant." As I started doing sketches, I tried to think of the things I most enjoy drawing, which I then made as extravagant and over the top as possible. Musclemen and tattoos came to mind because, after all, both muscles and tattoos are excessive vanities. From there it was just a matter of execution!

BENOIT
Decorating Mistakes

STEVE BRODNER
Sarah Palin

STEVE BRODNER
Ski Wisconsin

STEVE BRODNER
Clash of the Titans

Harry Campbell

Radical Islam

This was assigned by Brian Rea, former art director of *The New York Times* op-ed page, and a great creative mind to be working with. I always tried to do my absolutely best work for Brian, and the subject matter usually helped, since, more often than not, it was good, timely, and rich with possibilities. This piece was about how to deal with certain radical elements of Islam. The article talked about how, despite being crushed, various radical factions would inevitably strengthen and

regroup. I did a few solutions using the Islamic symbol of a crescent and a star, being very careful not to self-edit, but also being sensitive not to offend people of the Islamic faith. I could always count on Brian to either push the concept or how I handled it just a bit and get me to do my best work, or to leave it alone. Op-ed work is a thrill because the material is good and the deadline is tight.

DOUG CHAYKA

No Exit

The article by Daniel Lazare, which appeared in *The Nation*, begins by asking, "What does the Constitution mean?" and considers which rights, if any, are specifically guaranteed by the Constitution. We are left to wonder if the Constitution is anything more than a vague labyrinth in which any meaning can be found.

Doug Chayka

Ajax

For a review by Emily Wilson in *The Nation* of John Tipton's chilling translation of Sophocles's *Ajax*. This new version modernizes the language of the play and makes a clear connection to the Vietnam and Iraq wars.

MARCOS CHIN

The Safety Gap

I knew I wanted to keep this illustration graphic and simple, and, after reading the article, I already had in mind the theme of "Man versus Nature." The image was inspired by the story of Hanzel and Gretel leaving a trail of breadcrumbs to find their way back out of forest. I wanted to allude to the idea of FDA inspectors feeling lost and directionless when they enter China in search of drug manufacturing plants.

MARCOS CHIN

Hooters Road Trip

I was strangely excited when Rob Wilson called me for this project because I have never eaten at Hooters before. The article was about the author going on a two-week cross country road trip eating only at Hooters restaurants. The challenge was to try to make this restaurant scene more interesting and funny without being crass or obvious. The idea came to me after many failed versions of drawing the author traveling through a breast-like landscape filled with owls.

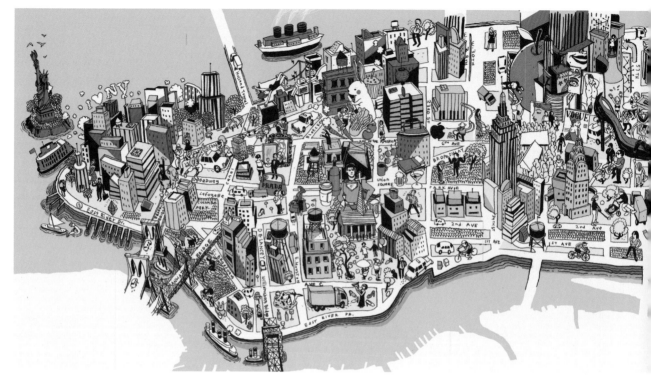

JOSH COCHRAN

Sexy City

Gatefold map of New York City with various points of interest from
the show *Sex and the City*. This map is an actual, accurate street map
of Manhattan.

JOSH COCHRAN
Natural Gas
A spread for *Fortune* magazine. Brian Hunter, a top trader for Amaranth, is blamed for destroying an $8 billion hedge fund. Hunter is now in the middle of a big war between the FERC and CFTC for control of regulation of the natural gas trading market.

JOHN CRAIG
Meatface

JOHN CUNEO
Charles Bukowski
A recently conducted, industry-wide poll has confirmed that the seven most favorable words a client can address to an illustrator are: "Give me a drawing of Charles Bukowski." Much credit goes to Nicholas Blechman for this deft bit of art direction.

FERNANDA COHEN

How Technology has Changed the Way We Live
This piece was commissioned by *Clarín*, the leading newspaper in Argentina, for Mother's Day. It was featured in a special section that focused on women, and the article was about how technology had changed the way we live, such as the way we read the news and shop online. The "1" and "0" symbolize a binary code.

Etienne Delessert

McCain's Suicide Wish
Since last September I have done a weekly page for the French satirical magazine *Siné Hebdo*. I am covering the American political scene for them. I have complete freedom to do whatever I want—no sketch—fun!

ETIENNE DELESSERT

McFaust

Also for the French satirical magazine *Siné Hebdo*. Clearly, at the end of their campaign, McCain and Sarah Palin crossed a dangerous line.

OLIVER DOMINGUEZ
Walking a Monk

RICHARD DOWNS
The Devil and Ronnie Marquez

A Phoenix man, involved in the bloody exorcism of his three-year-old granddaughter, died unexpectedly in the summer of 2007. Did police officers electrocute him, or was he the victim of his own demons? Art director Brian Goddard wanted to capture the chaos and the bloody scene without showing blood, so my use of black and red was a good approach. This was a three-part assignment and this scene depicts Cynthia, Ronnie's daughter, who was found in a corner clutching a photograph of the Pope. The autopsy report indicates Ronnie Marquez was tased 22 times.

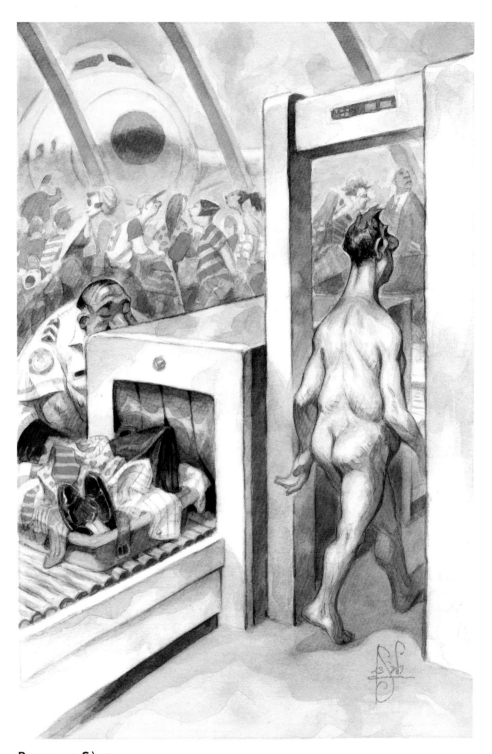

PETER DE SÈVE

Through the Wringer
I am proud to say that I have the singular distinction of having drawn both the very first and second naked butts ever to be published on the cover of *The New Yorker*.

BYRON EGGENSCHWILER

Portishead

At the start, the direction I was given, more than anything else, was to bring across the feel of Portishead's music. The idea for the gently swaying band evolved out of numerous sketches and scribbles I did while just listening to their music, waiting until something worked out and matched the mood I was looking for. There is a fragile and haunt- ing atmosphere within the band's songs that served here as my best source of reference and inspiration. Whenever I can preserve a little mystery in an image, I end up a bit happier about it in the end, and this was one of those cases. I treated the final with ink and ink washes, then compiled and colored in Photoshop.

ROBIN ELEY

Displacement

This painting for *Memphis* magazine accompanied the grand-prize-winning story from their 2007 Fiction Contest. Entitled "Tim Bui Blues," by Jackson McKenzie, the protagonist in the story struggles with the physical and emotional displacement caused by Hurricane Katrina. Desperate and depressed, he seeks comfort in the familiar: a tattered bathrobe, a captain's hat, and an old baseball almanac. Assailed by the unfamiliar, he seeks solitude in the one place where he can be alone—the bathroom. It is here that I have depicted him, close to drowning, lost in the memories of his life before the hurricane. Above the water-line are the trees that line the Mississippi River, where he used to while away the hours fishing. He is keeping his head above the water—just. Hopefully, the water will not rise any further before he learns to deal with his grief and find redemption. The art director was Hudd Byard.

THOMAS FUCHS
Mortar Keys
This piece is about professors at universities using their students to ghostwrite their papers/books for them. The image seeks to combine both of those elements, commenting on the subject without taking a specific position.

YVETTA FEDOROVA
Headstrong Historian
"Headstrong Historian" was created for the fiction section in *The New Yorker*. They wanted a very minimal approach. It was a beautiful story about three generations of strong African women trying to survive. I created my own jewelry and fabric designs based on Nigerian traditional designs.

YVETTA FEDOROVA
Gray Matters

Gray Matters was created for *American Lawyer* magazine. It is about baby boomers being fired from their CEO positions. I wanted to create a multi-layered effect combining flat colors with fabrics and real hair.

ALESSANDRO GOTTARDO
Year in Review
This was for a financial article about the balance of the year that had
passed (2007) and what we have to look for in the coming year (2008).

ALESSANDRO GOTTARDO

Roy Spivey 1 of 2
This was for a short story for *Internazionale*. It's about a middle-aged woman who's considering the lost chance she had in her youth to have a liaison with a famous actor she'd met on a plane.

EDDIE GUY
Esquire China Opener

These two images accompany an article by Colby Buzzell for *Esquire*. Shenzhen, once a Chinese fishing village now population eleven million, has become an experiment in Chinese capitalism. Colby explores the contradictions of East meeting West and the effects of enormous foreign investment in this runaway city. *Esquire* creative director, David Curcurito, was looking for propaganda imagery, combining elements of the old and new.

MICHAEL GLENWOOD
The Hidden Bars of New York

JASON HOLLEY
Ultra Marathon

The Heads of State

Los Angeles Magazine

A feature in *Los Angeles* magazine on the troubled state of *The Los Angeles Times* and the various owners that have come and gone over the years.

JODY HEWGILL
Putin's New Evil Empire
Art director Ingrid Shields commissioned me to do a portrait of Putin looking dodgy for a feature article in the launch issue of *Standpoint* magazine. Ingrid and the editor wanted me to find inspiration from the photos of a shirtless Putin as he posed for photographers while on a fishing expedition.

BRAD HOLLAND
Stealing Weather

STERLING HUNDLEY

The Gibson Girl

In many ways, the love life of Charles Dana Gibson and Irene Lang-horne mirrored that of Pygmato and Galeata from Greek mythology. Pygmato sculpted a woman of ivory. Falling in love with his creation, he prayed to Aphrodite to make her real. Aphrodite complied and breathed life into Galatea. Pygmato and Galeata wed and spent the rest of their lives in love. In 1895, Charles Dana Gibson married Irene Langhorne at Saint Paul's church (built in the Greek Revival style) in

Richmond, Virginia. Like Galatea before her, Irene Langhorne bore a striking resemblance to the artist's idealized beauty. Becoming Gibson's premiere model, Langhorne transitioned from Gibson's gal into the Gibson Girl and became the face of the first American pin-up. The Gibson Girl would remain in vogue until the outbreak of the First World War. Charles Dana Gibson and Irene Langhorne Gibson would spend the rest of their lives together, and in love.

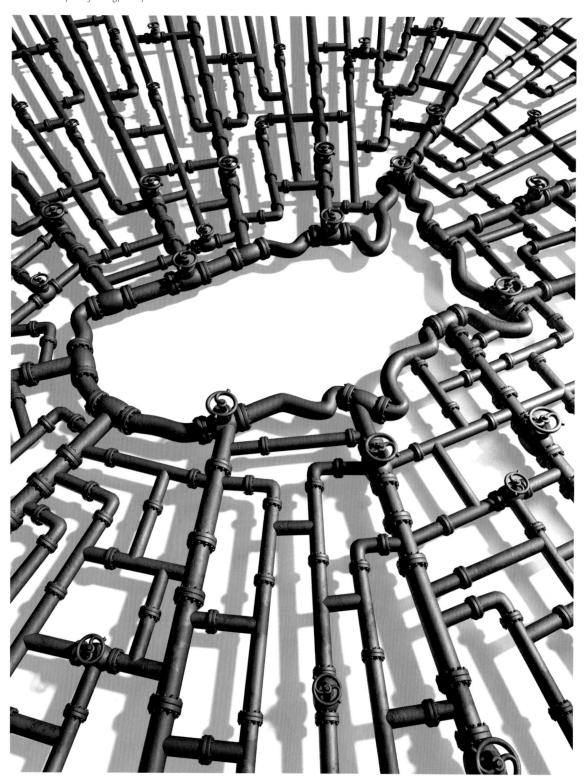

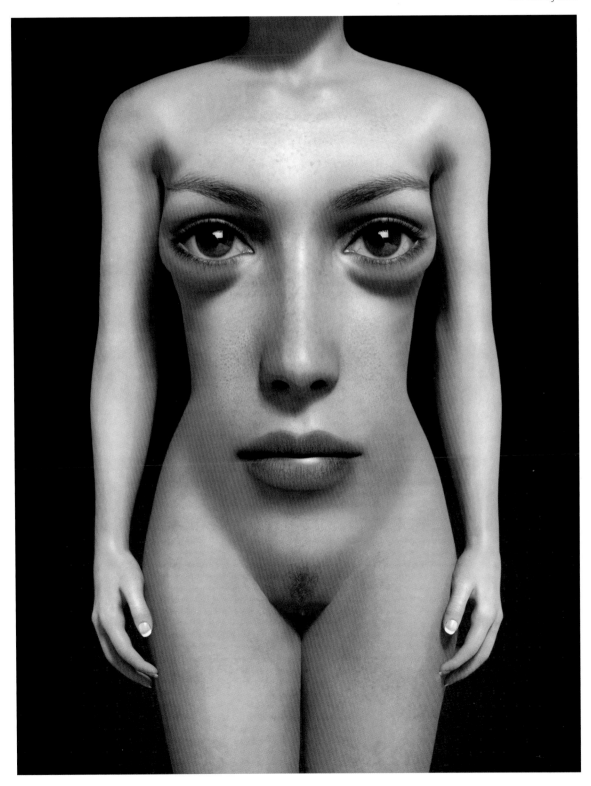

MARIKO JESSE
Ceramic Dim Sum

SATOSHI KAMBAYASHI

The Hillary Question

This is an illustration for the comment and opinion page of *The Guardian* newspaper in London, which I do every other week. This one was for the March 7, 2008, edition, in the middle of the heated 2008 Democratic primaries. It was about how Hillary Clinton's candidacy was causing conflict, generational collision, and soul-searching for American feminists. Should a woman support Clinton out of sisterly duty alone? She became a bit of a riddle to female voters, and the Tenniel image from Alice in Wonderland, where Alice confronts the Cheshire Cat, aptly demonstrated the situation, Hillary Clinton being the cat.

EDWARD KINSELLA
Metallica
This piece was for the review of Metallica's album: *Death Magnetic*.

EDWARD KINSELLA

The New Anxiety
The article for this assignment dealt with a recent increase in the number of Philadelphia police officers killed in the line of duty.

Tatsuro Kiuchi

Better Days
This was a cover illustration for an elder care magazine published in
Japan. I was asked to do a piece that had anything to do with everyday
lives. I came up with a train, which I think was a symbol of commuting.
The piece is digitally created with Photoshop.

TATSURO KIUCHI

The Traveler Into Books

This was originally created as a sketch for a *New York Times* article about traveling with four-legged friends. However, the idea was rejected since it was similar to another illustration they had used in the past. Eventually, it was selected to be published by Kadokawa in Japan as a magazine cover. The piece is digitally created with Photoshop.

SEAN KELLY

The Flatiron Building

The popular weekly column *Metropolitan Diary* in *The New York Times* provided a wonderful opportunity to play with my choice of the great visual icons of New York. On and off, over the course of two years, I created over 50 images about the city's classic sites and scenes, based on personal stories submitted by readers. Art director Michael Kolomatsky generously encouraged me to depart from these anecdotes and go off on a tangent—conceptually, to free associate, and to use the tales as a springboard—or, in this case, another kind of board.

TATSURO KIUCHI

It Never Is
This is a piece for the fiction series *Row 22 - Seats A&B* by Frederick Waterman in *Hemispheres*, United Airlines's inflight magazine. This time, the story was about Texas hold'em in Las Vegas. The piece is digitally created with Photoshop.

PRICE $4.99

OCT. 22, 2007

THE NEW YORKER

LORENZO MATTOTTI
Unmasked Beauty

JASON MUNN
The $55 Trillion Question

ALEX NABAUM

Windpower

This piece for *This Old House* magazine introduced an article for homeowners interested in setting up a wind turbine on their property. The writer touched on various points about carbon, do-it-yourself options, and the fact that the homeowner would be a pioneer. I made sure I did a wide variety of roughs to cover any emphasis, from general to specific. Some of the roughs were a pioneer wagon, carbon dragon, and even an *American Gothic* spoof. Hylah Hill, the art director on this job, wisely went with the more general and broader concept sketch of the outlet face.

CHRIS SILAS NEAL
Obama, Lion Tamer

TIM O'BRIEN

The Last Empire

Perhaps no current magazines use more illustration than *PlanSponsor*, *Runner's World*, and *Mother Jones*. For this cover, Tim Luddy asked me to revisit the famous movie poster of the *Last Emperor* and update the boy. Easy assignment but a hard image to paint. In the end, the cover reflected the main article's question: Can the world survive China's headlong rush to emulate the American way of life?

DAVID PLUNKERT
Making Credit Safer: The Case for Regulation
Illustration for an article about avoiding mortgage credit traps.

DAVID PLUNKERT

Cold Friends, Wrapped in Mink and Medals
Portrait of Vladimir Putin for an article about Russia's military routing
of Georgia.

EMILIANO PONZI

Burnout

The article was about burnout at the CFO level. The turnover rate for CFOs has increased by 100% in the past year, so I thought the image of a match slowly fizzling out illustrated the idea. Meanwhile, the matchbook in the background is filled with matches ready to replace each other, one by one.

CHRIS RAHN

The Rat Ladies

This piece was done for an article in the *L.A. Weekly* about two older women, identical twin sisters, who live in Beverly Hills and have caused untold damage to their upscale neighborhood by feeding the rats they found on their property. Apparently the rat population exploded as a result of their actions. Art director Derek Rainey and I decided to go for a feeling that was a mix of rigid formality and utter creepiness.

THILO ROTHACKER
The Staircase

GRAHAM ROUMIEU
Feed the Squirrels

This piece accompanied a letter in *The Globe and Mail*, wherein a man defended his right to feed neighborhood squirrels, much to the chagrin of his non-squirrel-loving neighbors. Perhaps not Pulitzer worthy, but fun. I twice came across the piece clipped out of the paper, once at a coffee shop and again at a bookstore where employees had personalized the piece by adding glasses and different hairdos to make the character more in their own likeness.

STEPHEN SAVAGE
Portrait of Ted Turner

Ted Turner was my first ever commissioned needlepoint portrait. *Atlanta* magazine design director Eric Caposella had seen my uncommissioned portrait of Steve Heller (a Gold Medal winner in the Society of Illustrators 50th Annual) and a Bill Clinton on my website, and thought the home-spun medium would suit the billionaire philanthropist perfectly. The full-page assignment came in just as I was headed up to Vermont with my wife for a week's vacation. Normally, I might have cut the vacation short in order to complete the job. But instead, I found myself sitting in a comfy chair in front of a crackling fire for four hours a night in our cozy cabin, stitching away. Thankfully, needlepoint travels well! These needlepoint faces always begin as simple drawings on tracing paper. I transfer the drawing to a grid (using Photoshop) then count out the location of each square on plastic mesh as I stitch back and forth with acrylic yarn.

OTTO STEININGER

Think Tank

I don't remember too much detail about this article other than that it was discussing think tanks. My memory escapes me probably because my mind was elsewhere that day: I had a bicycle accident and was wondering whether I had contracted any permanent damage to my hand and elbow. I got "doored" again by a parked car. Needless to say, since I was in a lot of pain, I was hoping and praying that the concept got approved without hitches. It did. So this was a painless painful day at work.

YUKO SHIMIZU
Measuring a Bear

FRANK STOCKTON
Bad Blood

PRICE $4.50　　THE　　FEB. 25, 2008

NEW YORKER

ADRIAN TOMINE

Shelf Life

JONATHAN TWINGLEY
Yes, We're Open

"Yes, We're Open" could mean a lot of things these days. It's a tricky time. This painting was made for a magazine called *The Deal*, which isn't available on newsstands and that's a shame because it's one of the best publications I've ever worked for, largely because of Larry Gendron, the art director there. If every magazine had a Larry Gendron, more magazines would still be able to say, Yes, we're open.

JACK UNRUH

Basso Matic

TJ Tucker called: "Jack I have the perfect job for you." And it was! The state of Texas does research on bass over 13lbs. that are caught by fishermen on Texas lakes. They are picked up live and transported to the lab in Athens, Texas. Some research photos I did 20 years ago for a Biotech annual report came in handy as authentic-looking lab stuff.

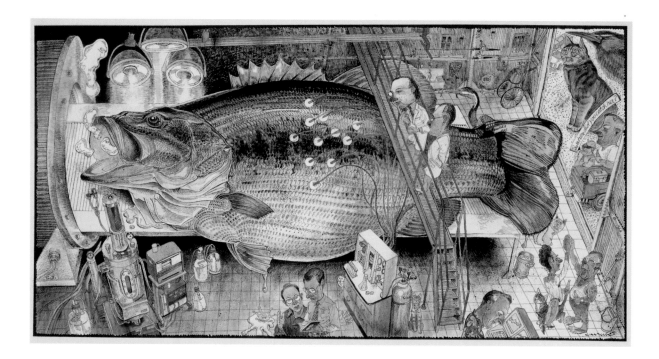

JACK UNRUH
Giuliani

New York magazine needed a quick portrait of Rudy. He was withdrawing from the race for president. My directions were to have him look sad. I've done some sad portraits in my time.

RICHARD WILLIAMS
Thanksgiving with the Stars

ADVERTISING/INSTITUTIONAL

JULIETTE BORDA
ILLUSTRATOR

Juliette Borda has been creating award-winning illustrations for book publishers, magazines, newspapers, and corporate publications for over 16 years. In 2009 her gouache paintings were selected for a traveling show entitled "Picturing Health," which originated at the Norman Rockwell Museum, and is traveling to Ireland, Turkey, Iceland, the UK, and France. In addition, her work was included in the Exquisite Book Project, published by Chronicle, which features the work of 100 contemporary fine artists, illustrators, designers, and comic artists. She lives and works in New York City.

SOOJIN BUZELLI
CREATIVE DIRECTOR, ASSET INTERNATIONAL

SooJin Buzelli is an award-winning art director/designer at Asset International in Stamford, CT, which publishes *PLANSPONSOR* and *PLAN-ADVISER* magazines. SooJin has been art directing and designing magazines, events, and conferences for the more than 12 years since she graduated from Rhode Island School of Design with an Illustration BFA. Her love for illustration shines in each of her publications, which are filled with some of the most highly skilled and freshest talent in the field. She has been recognized for her art direction and design work from organizations such as the Society of Publication Designers (SPD), the Society of Illustrators, *Communication Arts*, *Print*, *3x3*, and *American Illustration*. SooJin also teaches an illustration class at School of Visual Arts, and lives in the East Village with her husband Chris and their dog Sota.

FRANCES JETTER
ILLUSTRATOR

Since 1974, Frances Jetter's work has appeared in many publications, including *The New York Times*, *The Washington Post*, *Time*, *The Village Voice*, *The Nation*, and *The Progressive*. She illustrated books for The Franklin Library, ads for Audubon, and book jackets for Knopf, Macmillan, and others. Her work is in the collections of the Fogg Art Museum at Harvard University, Detroit Institute of Arts, and The New York Public Library Print Collection.

She received a fellowship from New York Foundation for the Arts in 2003. Awards and annuals include *Graphis*, *Print*, the Society of Illustrators, *American Illustration*, *Communication Arts*, and the Society of Publication Designers. She is on the Illustrator's Advisory Board of the Norman Rockwell Museum, and has taught at the School of Visual Arts since 1979.

JOHN KASCHT
ILLUSTRATOR

John Kascht's carefully observed satirical portraits have appeared in newspapers, books, magazines, and theater windows for 25 years. He has received awards from the Society of Illustrators, *American Illustration*, *Communication Arts*, and Gold and Silver Medals from the Society of Publication Designers and The Society of Newspaper Design. John lives and works on a small farm in Northeastern Pennsylvania. When not drawing funny portraits of famous people, he can be found boiling maple sap into syrup, splitting wood, and helping his wife tend her beehives.

KENNA KAY
VP/CREATIVE DIRECTOR,
TV LAND MTV

Kenna Kay is the v.p./creative
director at TV Land, a division
of MTV Networks Entertainment Group. Previously, she
was art director at Nickelodeon. Her work has been
recognized by Promax/BDA,
Print, *Communication Arts*,
HOW, The Art Directors Club,
and D&AD. She has spoken
on design issues for AIGA,
the How Conference, the
University of Kansas, the University of Wisconsin, The Art
Director's Club, and in Cara-
cas, Venezuela. Her judging
experience includes *American
Illustration*, 365 AIGA "Year
in Design," and various local
and regional shows. Kenna
served on the New York board
of AIGA, where she organized
the "MOVE: Design for Film
and Television" conference.
She currently serves on the
national board of AIGA. She
teaches in the Illustration
Department at Parsons the
New School For Design.

INA SALTZ
ART DIRECTOR, DESIGNER

Ina Saltz is an art director,
designer, design critic, photographer, and professor (at
CCNY) who specializes in
typography and magazine
design. For over 22 years, she
was the design director for
such publications as *Time*
magazine's international
editions, *Worth* magazine,
BusinessWeek, *Golf* magazine,
and *Worldbusiness* magazine.
Ina is on the design faculty
of the Stanford Publishing
Course; she has also taught
"virtually" for Stanford via
webcast. Since 2002 Ina has
been a regular columnist for
STEP Inside Design magazine,
and also writes for *HOW* and
others. Ina's first book, *BODY
TYPE: Intimate Messages
Etched in Flesh* for Abrams
Books, is in its third printing.
In 2009, Abrams will publish
volume two of *BODY TYPE*,
and her third book, *Typography Essentials: 100 Design Prin-
ciples for Working with Type*,
will be published in 2009 by
Rockport Press.

MICHAEL SLOAN
ILLUSTRATOR

Michael Sloan spent several
years working as a printmaker
in Paris, France, and Venice,
Italy, before moving to New
York City. His illustrations first
appeared on the Op-Ed page
of *The New York Times*, where
he remains a frequent contributor to the Letters column.
He has created illustrations
for many clients, including
Fortune, *The Village Voice*, *The
New Yorker*, Barnes & Noble,
The American Prospect, and
The San Francisco Chronicle.
Michael is the author of the
Professor Nimbus books and
comics. His second graphic
novel, *The Heresy of Professor
Nimbus*, was awarded a Silver
Medal in the Society of Illustrators 49th Annual. Michael
also plays bass guitar with the
all-illustrators jazz band, The
Half-Tones.

JAMES VICTORE
DESIGNER

James Victore's clients include
Moet & Chandon, Aveda,
Apple, Fuse TV, *Time*, Yohji
Yamamoto, Yamaha, *The New
York Times*, and the School of
Visual Arts. With two friends,
he has a design workshop:
Sahre Victore Wilker. He
has designed original, hand-
painted surfboards for Design
Within Reach. Awards include
an Emmy for TV animation, a
Gold Medal from the Broadcast Designers Association,
the Grand Prix from the Brno
(Czech Republic) Biennale,
and Gold and Silver Medals
from The New York Art Directors Club. Victore's designs
are in the permanent collections of the Palais du Louvre,
Paris; the Library of Congress,
Washington, DC; the Design
Museum, Zurich; the Stedelijk
Museum, Amsterdam; and
MoMA is exhibiting five of his
posters. His work is featured
in magazines around the
world, and a monograph of
his work will be out in 2010.
He teaches graphic design at
the School of Visual Arts.

Leaf Man
This is an ad for an Ashtanga Yoga studio, Tokyo-yoga.com. The message is that by taking their Ashtanga yoga classes—the toughest yoga for body and mind—you are both mentally and physically fulfilled to be the real you. The poster was first drawn with a pencil then with black and red pens only. I was passionate about creating an ad that nobody had ever seen before. I concentrated on expressing the authentic world of yoga in a truly unique illustration. It took me many rounds until I could achieve this flat yet consistent look of illustration that completely eliminates 3D elements.

Western Tanager
Celestial Seasonings is a company best known for high quality tea, and the memorable and creative art adorning their tea boxes. When they decided to expand their product line to include organic coffee, I was asked to create the initial five packages. The main direction was to emphasize the flavor and natural coffee-growing environment, without the whimsical elements I typically design in my tea illustrations. I had a very strong and simple vision for this piece, knowing that I wanted it to be atmospheric yet intimate and "jewel-like." I must confess, after I found out that I won my first medal from the Society of Illustrators after nearly 25 years as an illustrator, I regarded it as an award for surviving so long. Then I realized that it just makes me want to be better—and boosts my energy for the next 25! I am eternally honored by this special recognition.

Twins
Dave Plunkert of Spur Design asked me to create the cover for Serbin Communication's promotional brochure, on the theme "Putting Your Best Face Forward." The "half" on the left was on the cover, the "half" on the right was revealed when you opened the booklet.

CHRIS BUZELLI

Tropen Poster: Golden Java Demon Statue

What is your dream job? I could not have thought this one up in my wildest dreams. I was commissioned by Saatchi & Saatchi to work on a series of posters for the Tropenmuseum in Amsterdam. They had five new artifacts and wanted to illustrate the story behind each artifact. This particular painting was for a 14th century golden statue from Eastern Java. It depicts an ancient poem about a demon king and a Buddha-prince on a journey to enlightenment. The tale is full of ancestral kingdoms, palaces, cannibalism, and princesses.

As You Like It
I was commissioned to create posters for the entire season of plays at Soulpepper Theater in Toronto, a total of eight images. This painting was used as the poster for William Shakespeare's *As You Like It*. The play is very complex so I went through a lot of thumbnails trying to find an iconic image that would work for the poster. I kept going back to a scene in the play where a character who kills a deer wears the animal's skin and horns over his own head. The art director for the entire project was Anthony Swaneveld.

Burlesque Dancers
The Queen Street studio is a not-for-profit rehearsal space for theatre and dance, run by a friend of mine. To stay afloat, they have an auction of works by people they know. Last year they had these two young burlesques dancers performing before the bidding started. They juggled barrels with their feet, balanced on objects, and spun and twirled things—all while wearing not much. This is my remembered version of them a year later. They were at the auction again this year and put in the winning bid for the print.

Honky Tonk Spring
Honky Tonk Spring was created for a Toronto art exhibit called "1st Sign of Spring." Sixteen illustrators addressed a single idea and presented personal interpretations of the season. The idea of spring foliage sprouting from a country western outfit came to me while looking at a picture of songwriter Gram Parsons. In the photograph, Parsons wears a suit appliquéd with flowing cannabis leaves. The suit was designed by Nudie Cohn, known for creating wonderfully elaborate rhinestone-covered outfits for entertainers. Inside each of the flowers in my illustration, I portrayed icons of sin and folly also inspired by imagery emblazoned on Parsons' Nudie suit.

Recollect—
Dead Custom Vans Show
A printed piece and a custom pair of Vans sneakers were featured in a group show at Cave Gallery in Detroit. The show loosely blended the spirit of Halloween and traditions of Day of the Dead with sneaker and snowboard culture.

MONIKA AICHELE
The Excursions of Mr.Broucek

Fred Muenzmaier and Andrea Schroeder, in the art department of Deutsche Grammophon, wanted me to do a CD cover illustration for the opera *The Excursions of Mr. Broucek* by Leos Janacek. For my inspiration they sent me old posters advertising the opera and information about the setting of the story—Mr. Broucek's real world and his imaginary trips to the moon. It took me several sketches to bring these scenarios together and give them a surreal touch. The illustration has been seen by Junko Kajikawa, of the Tokyo Symphonic Orchestra, who loved it a lot and asked me to adapt it for the orchestra's promotion material.

KELLY ALDER
Popidiot Catalogue Cover

PATRICK ARRASMITH

Eaglepus

This image was created as part of a group of illustrations to showcase the advertising agency's different qualities that allow them to handle all manner of projects. I was just happy to draw this bizarre creature with an eagle's head and an octopus's body riding the waves. The next image might have him flying through the skies on tentacled wings. I'm still waiting for that commission.

MARK BENDER

Only Me

This piece was a poster to promote an original musical about a single, selfless 30-something social worker dedicated to her needy family. With the support of her father, she finally puts herself first and finds love.

KAKO BERGAMINI
The Trial
Kafka's *The Trial* was one of three pieces for Companhia das Letras's pocket book collection campaign. The idea was to graphically insert an object that one could fit in a pocket into each book cover scenario.

Marc Burckhardt

When Problems Are a Joy

Weiden-Kennedy/London asked me to create a series of paintings that played off the theme "When Problems Are a Joy," underscoring Honda's engineering innovation using the analogy of puzzle solving. The ads were placed throughout the transportation system in London as a kind of game for the idle viewer to solve. They led to a website, which is found on the pencil shaft. (Look closely!)

MARC BURCKHARDT

Frank's Hot Sauce

A great project and a wonderful use of illustration. Tony Larsen at EuroRSCG wanted to convey the heat of Frank's Hot Sauce, and had a sense of humor about how to do it. Bosch wasn't available, but I was glad to step in!

CHRIS BUZELLI

Tropen Poster: Jainism Golden Altar Statue

I was commissioned by Saatchi & Saatchi to work on a series of posters for the Tropenmuseum in Amsterdam. They had five new artifacts and wanted to illustrate the story behind each artifact. This painting was for a Jainism alter piece symbolizing emptiness. Jainism is an ancient Indian religion. The goal for Jain members is to leave earth and to reach Dharma/Nirvana. The altarpiece was used in their meditation to purify their souls and disconnect from the material world.

CHRIS BUZELLI

Tropen Poster: Ghana Fish Coffin

This was also one of the posters for the Tropenmuseum in Amsterdam. It illustrates the story behind a wooden coffin shaped like a fish from Ghana, circa 2000. The people from Ghana honor their dead with brightly-colored, hand-carved wooden coffins that celebrate the way they lived. The coffins are designed to represent an aspect of the dead person's life, such as a car if one was a driver, a hammer for a carpenter, or a fish for a fisherman.

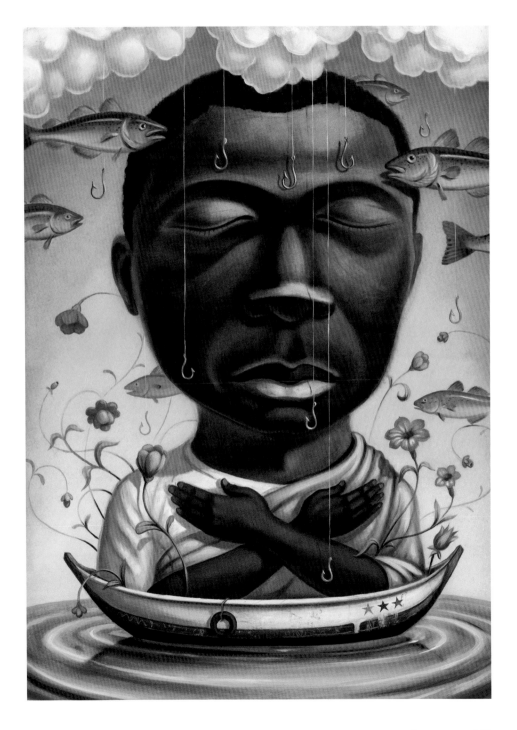

CHRIS BUZELLI

United Poster: Great Wall Dragon

This painting was commissioned for a United Airlines ad campaign to promote their new flights to Beijing that coincided with the Beijing Olympics. This was one of four dragon illustrations for the campaign and each dragon had to have a different look. I really enjoyed researching the history and discovering the variety of dragons used in Chinese art.

CHRIS BUZELLI
United Poster: Koi Dragon
This painting was also for the United Airlines ad campaign to promote their new flights to Beijing that coincided with the Beijing Olympics. It was based on an old Chinese fable in which a koi achieves its goal through hard work and becomes a magical dragon when it reaches the top of the waterfall. The illustration appeared on billboards, magazines, airline tickets, and as an inflight screen animation.

DOUG BOEHM

Fragility Returns to Nature

A band from the UK commissioned me to create this illustration for their first CD entitled *You Are Goldmouth*. The music is based on the story of Goldmouth, which is about returning to nature and knowing your true self. Vulnerability and self-awareness was a large part of the concept. I've painted the anatomical muscle man in previous personal works. He functions as a metaphor for fragility. The final illustration turned out to be more of a personal piece than a commissioned illustration.

MARA CERRI
Calm 2

HARRY CAMPBELL
Workbook Divider

I got a call from *Workbook*'s Tommy Steel to do a divider spread for the popular source book. This was a pro bono piece, with the added bonus of a free spread in the workbook. And I was allowed to do anything I wanted. I'd been dying to do more personal work, particularly these sorts of constructed faces—ones that were recognizable as faces but not too goofy or robot-like. I was also interested in the idea of composi-tions of random elements coming together. I love looking at exploded views of anything—washing machines, car engines, anything—stuff that I think would bore most artists. I just love the mechanical certainty of it all, but also the chaotic complexity. This was a step in that direction, something I would like to explore a bit more. It was also an oppor-tunity to explore new color directions, or, as it were, less color.

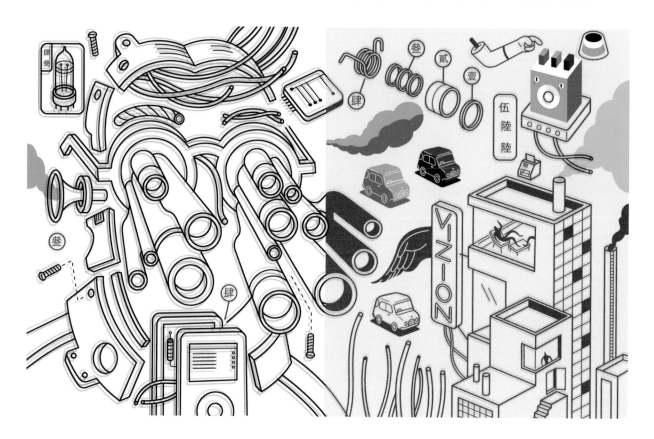

HARRY CAMPBELL

Parts Face

This was assigned by David Plunkert at Spur Design as part of a promotional mailer for the *Directory of Illustration*. The only direction I was given was that it had to be a face or have something to do with a face. I don't really do many portraits per say—the occasional likeness assignment, but not my regular thing. I handed in a few ideas of more realistic faces, split faces, he/she type things but I felt most strongly about this idea and fortunately so did David. This was a pro-bono assignment with the added bonus of a free page in the source book and a great deal of creative freedom, which allowed me to do some exploration, something I don't always get a chance to do in my day-to-day work. I love drawing simple objects—radio tubes, nuts, bolts, wires, things you would see in an old Craftsman users guide—that type of thing. These objects are inanimate but I think that's what I like about them. They're devoid of emotion, but string a few of them together and they begin to be something else.

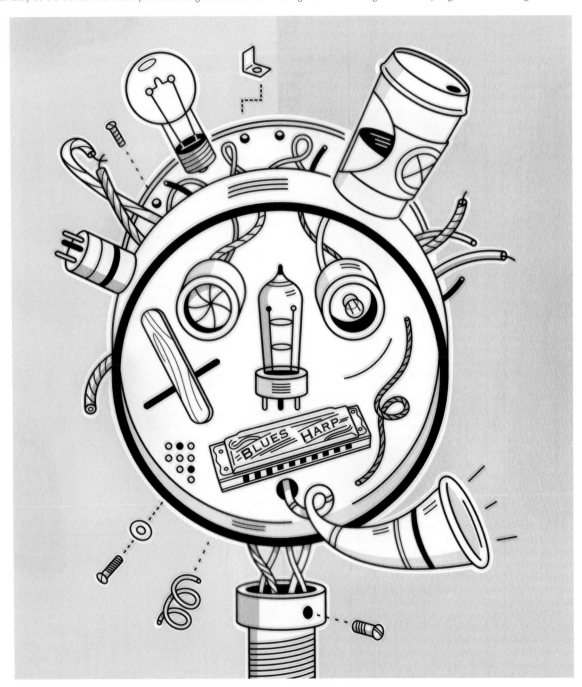

DOUG CHAYKA

100% Wrong
The Ne'ers describe their music as "fifty percent heavy thoughts and fifty percent knee-jerk reactions with a sound best described as full-on in-your-face visceral mooning, a distillation of art, alcohol and attitude—not only intoxicating but mind-numbing in a good way." I put on the rough mixes, started drawing, and this is what I came up with for the cover art.

JOSH COCHRAN
Corridors of Blood
Illustration for a book on the early American Express cardholders. This is about Richard Gordon, an early horror film producer who often collaborated with legends like Boris Karloff and horror director Antony Balch. The illustration is titled after one of Karloff's early films, *Corridors of Blood*.

SARAH J. COLEMAN

Sing for Change

The "Sing...Change" campaign brings together British Girl Guides (the UK's Girl Scouts) to share their vocal talents while helping girls in Nepal gain access to water through the UK's Water Aid campaign. Often, women and children are those worst affected by poor sanitation, bearing the burden of collecting water and caring for relatives. Created in colored inks on paper, this illustration was an absolute pleasure to do, and communicates the joy of singing to bring about change!

SARAH J. COLEMAN
Sky High Hopes

Created for The Outfit's range of 2009 Tote Bags, this is part of their Environmental range. Since I create my best work around words and stories, I commissioned the copy from writer Ed Garland, who supplied lots of tiny phrases and stories for the project. This one grabbed me straightaway, prompting the pencils into inspired action! The piece is hand-drawn in ink, at 12 inches square, and colored up digitally for a clean, screen-printable look.

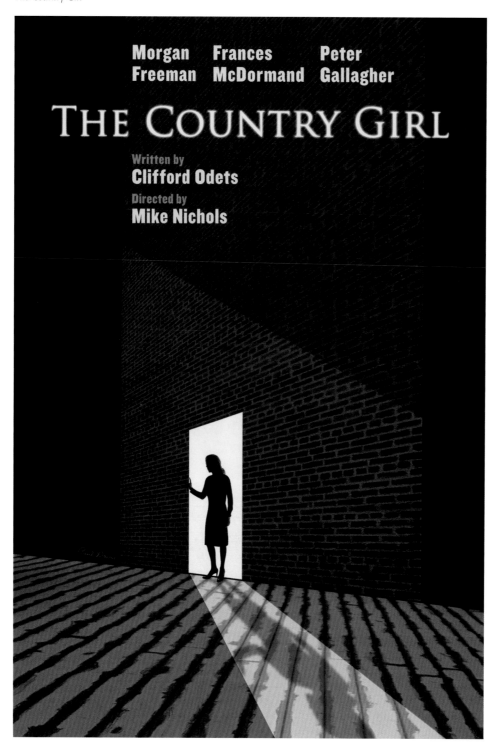

GIANNI DE CONNO
Glass Menagerie

ETIENNE DELESSERT

Carnaval Literario
Every year, this incredibly progressive school in Valencia, Spain, (with students age 1-18) organizes a literary and arts festival with a theme. Last year it was Noah's Ark revisited.

ISABELLE DERVAUX

Les Viennoiseries

This is the third postcard in a series of three that included "The Petits Gateaux" and "The Patisseries," created for La Boulange, the popular café and bakery in San Francisco. The unique appeal of La Boulange is its mixture of authentic French and relaxed West Coast atmosphere. Pascal Rigo, the owner, asked me to create these postcards to familiarize his customers with the French names of their pastries.

OLIVER DOMINGUEZ
Ice Cream Lovers

LEO ESPINOSA

Pombo Musical CD Cover and Poster
A CD cover/poster for a multi-platform music and literary project, designed for children to rediscover the characters and fables by Rafaél Pombo, Colombia's premiere children's writer from the turn of the last century.

MAX ESTES
Vote for Change Poster

The client (SS+K) phoned me on a Tuesday afternoon around 4:00. Would I like to design a poster for the Obama presidential campaign? I replied without hesitation, "Yes!!" Great. I would have until Friday morning to produce the image. The assignment came and went so fast, I hardly had time to ponder missing the mark. Of course, it helped that I felt passionately about the subject matter. The image needn't be complex; the message was clear. Voting gives voice. My image was done Thursday evening and approved Friday morning.

SARA FANELLI
Wine Tour Poster

JAMES FIORENTINO

Black Vulture

The original watercolor painting measuring 11 by 14 inches was commissioned by The Raptor Trust of New Jersey, which rehabilitates wild birds and educates people about the importance of the species. The Raptor Trust was looking to create artwork that would be used for their website and media-related items. Other hawk paintings I created will be displayed in traveling shows to educate and raise money for the Trust. The inspiration for the artwork came from my own, up-close study of these birds, as well as many photo references. I chose the Black Vulture because this bird of prey has beautiful grace and is most often seen soaring along highways. I created a portrait of the bird from an unusual angle in order to have it flow off the side of the page, and to accentuate the detail and texture of the bird's face.

DOUGLAS FRASER

Mustang Ride

Art done for the Ford Canada motor company. A number of illustrators were assigned a model of a Ford car to interpret. The artwork was not to show the car, but to create an environment that expressed the personality of that particular model. The model I was assigned was the Mustang. I saw the streetlights as a runway for the car to strut its stuff. The final art was done as a black-and-white painting, then I added digital color sampled from a Mustang car.

YOKO FURUSHO

Dancing in a Minefield
This image is for the album cover of *Plushgun* and for their promotional materials. I'm really, really happy that my piece was selected for this competition. Thank you very much!

NICK GAETANO

Bella

This project came from Timothy Harris Design in San Francisco. Jeanette Aramburu is the art director. Jeanette had seen several of my landscape paintings and wanted something similar for a wine label project. After a phone discussion of the painting, she sent me an email with maybe 20 reference photos of Italy: vineyards, fields, houses, hills, etc. She also sent jpegs of a few of my landscape paintings that worked well with the label idea. I did some pencil sketches and then the painting. I had to repaint the sky three times; it was too texturally active at first. Then it became a blend of two colors, then just the single color it is now.

CHRIS GALL
When Good Flies Go Bad
This artwork was created for a printer who annually produces a calendar with frog themes. The artists were able to do whatever they wished. Since flies are often the victims in the fly/frog relationship, I chose to turn the tables on the frog community.

VON GLITSCHKA

Tickles the Clown

I was asked to create a poster design for a speaking engagement at an advertising college, and was told to do whatever I wanted. So, of course, I decided to do an evil clown named Tickles. My turnaround time was about 24 hours, so, as usual, I drew out my base art until it was refined and I knew exactly what I needed to do. I scanned it in and used it as my foundation to create the digital illustration. Tickles creeps most people out and that alone made the poster very effective for grabbing people's attention and scaring small children.

ALESSANDRO GOTTARDO

W Under Ful World
An advertising poster and catalog campaign about scuba fish hunting. The image represents a man hiding in the deep sea, looking for spectacular fishes.

RUDY GUTIERREZ
Western Union Mural

JESSIE HARTLAND
Kiewit Billboard
For one of a series of public service announcement billboards commissioned to four different artists, I was given a slogan to promote family togetherness. The client is a foundation in the Midwest and the message is to encourage people to turn off the TV and talk during dinner.

LINDA FENNIMORE

Thurgood

In a portrait of a celebrated actor portraying a popular figure, one should resemble the other without caricaturing either. This seemed easily done when Thurgood Marshall was to be played by James Earl Jones. Using Jones's graying hair and the distinctively heavy frames of Marshall's glasses, I was able to create a Jonesian Marshall. But the poster became more challenging once Lawrence Fishburne replaced Jones, and I was told to lose both glasses and gray. A high forehead and moustache didn't do the job, until I was able to capture Marshall's intensity. It is attitude more than facial features that gave me my Fishburnian Marshall.

Paul Hoppe

Destinations

The advertising agency Finest|Magma in Karlsruhe, Germany, invited me to contribute to a promotional agenda/calendar. The theme was "Ziele," which translates to both "goals" and "destinations." I decided to create a series of images that revolve around imaginary cityscapes and transportation. *Destinations* was the first of the series. I constructed the perspective while I was figuring out the composition on the actual piece, without doing any thumbnails. On top of that grid I created the specific architectural elements. The inking was done with brush and dip pen, and the coloring is digital.

BRAD HOLLAND
Third Eye

STERLING HUNDLEY

Sweet Bird of Youth

This piece was created as the poster for Arena Stage's production of *Sweet Bird of Youth* by Tennessee Williams. I distilled the story into a commentary on time and the effect of age on the three main characters. Chance Wayne is a handsome young man who has left his hometown behind in hopes of becoming a movie star. Princess Kosmonopolis, a famous actress, is fleeing from her recent Hollywood debut, which she thought was a flop. And Heavenly Finley, Chance Wayne's first true love,

was left diseased from one of Chance's many indiscretions in his attempt to climb to the top. Cathleen Tefft was the art director on the piece. After quite a few sketches, we went forward with the idea of pairing Princess's Hollywood glamour photo next to her rapidly aging hands. I kept thinking of *The Portrait of Dorian Gray* by Oscar Wilde. Visually, I wanted to depict Princess Kosmonopolis's frail, ancient hands, their texture, and their failing attempt to hold on to Chance.

JOHN KACHIK
Tom and Sally's Chocolate Cowboys

This is an image created for a faux country music CD case that actually contains a solid chocolate CD. I was sent a few samples of the chocolate with the printed cases; my daughters Emily and Isabel tell me they were delicious. Art director Carol Ross asked me to draw two singing cowboys, one with a guitar and one with a banjo, sitting on a fence. I could imagine the two as she described her vision of the image. Other than asking me to close one of the singer's eyes to better demonstrate his intensity, there were no changes from the original sketch. Brilliant art direction, really adding a lot to the character's feel and final image. Once the sketch was approved, the hand drawing was scanned and colored using Photoshop.

GWENDA KACZOR
Aspens
Coldwater Creek commissioned me to create this illustration, which was used in window displays for their Fall 2008 campaign. The artwork was subsequently used for other marketing materials as well, including the cover of their fall catalogue, prints throughout their stores, and in print and online advertising.

TATSURO KIUCHI
The Snow Angel
This image was used for the shopping bag for Starbucks Holiday Campaign 2007, "Pass the Cheer." Since the illustration was going to be printed on brown colored paper, I was asked to use only black, red, blue, white, and green in separate layers in Photoshop.

ROMAN KLONEK

Soy Joy Bike

I was selected to do two ads for the Soyjoy "Fortified with Optimism" campaign. The key words for the illustrations were happy, fun, optimism, etc. In this case they wanted a funny bicycle ride. The feeling of fun increases if you have a little group of good-tempered guys. So here they are: the funny four on their way down the hill. In the end, again. I did some masks in Photoshop and filled them up with woodcut texture.

BILL MAYER

Never Stop Thinking

This simple little light drawing all originated from Joe Albert's headline "Never stop thinking." This version was obvious, piling all of the little people of the team inside one head, all working collaboratively to get out of bed and put on those shoes and walk down the stairs and make coffee.

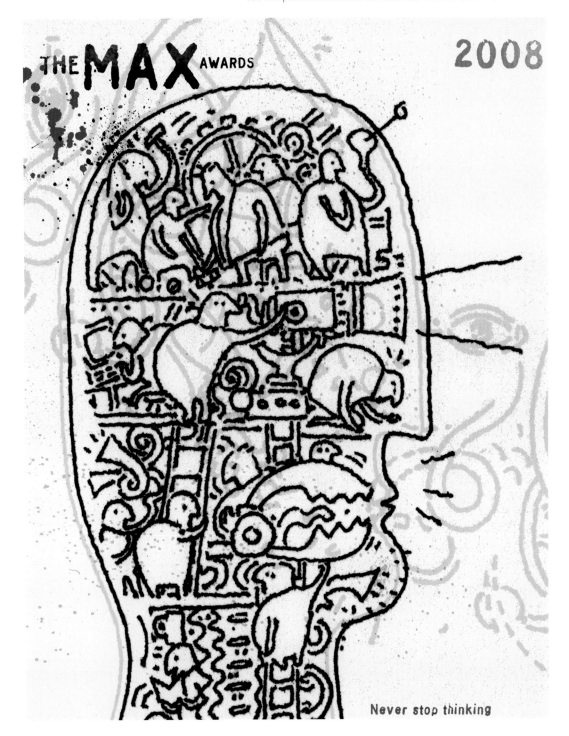

BILL MAYER
Pest Planet

This cover illustration started off as a one-page, reuse comic strip and morphed its way into kind of an underground comic, telling a tale of world domination by bugs going on an unchecked eating frenzy across Europe. Although the message of world domination certainly got played down in the final working copy, I guess they are still sensitive about world domination after sixty plus years.

BILL MAYER

Bug Reading Newspaper

This is one of the inside illustrations reusing the same bug as in *Pest Planet*, but this time it's reading *The Daily Bug* newspaper headline, "Productivity falls on EU farms." I love the copy Robert Roth wrote, in all of its changing variations. He made it easy to work back and forth on visuals. I ended up stripping these onto layered old paper I'd scanned to give the images an old comic feel.

GRADY MCFERRIN
Decemberists

This was a limited edition print commissioned by the Decemberists for a set of shows in Washington, DC. They asked several artists to make commemorative posters for different venues on their U.S. tour. The common theme was "Knights vs. Dear" (whatever that means). They were printed by Kayrock Screenprinting in Brooklyn.

AARON MESHON
NYC: Open Book

I created this piece for NYC and Company. It was so cool and inspiring to make an ad for the city I have called home for 14 years. I remember we only had about three weeks from start to finish on this. I gave them two sketches and they picked this one, with just some minor tweaks. I painted it in acrylic at about two-feet tall. I usually paint on watercolor paper and stretch it over a board so I can layer the acrylic without it warping. I was really inspired to put a lot of detail in the final, as I knew they were going to blow this up for subway ads in Europe and the U.S.A.

ROBERT MEGANCK

Ride the Blinds

The title *Ride the Blinds*, for the Sheryl Warner and the Southside Home-wreckers' CD, comes from the phrase that was used to describe the process of hitching a ride in an open boxcar.

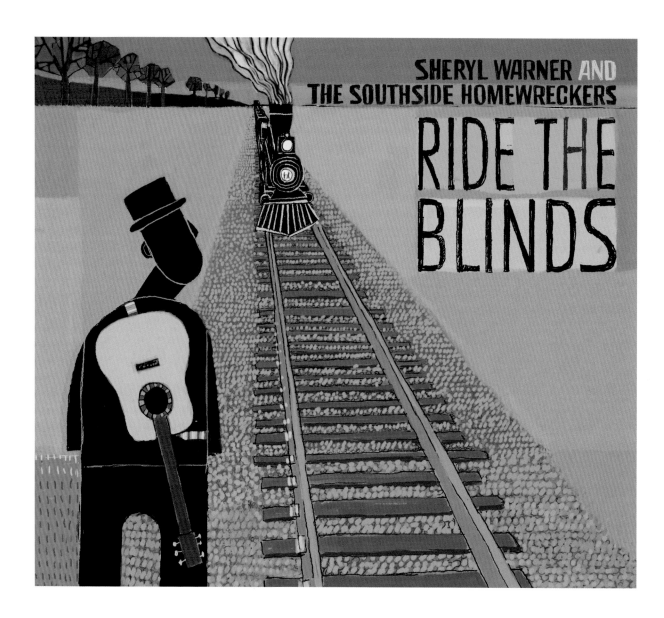

ROBERT MEGANCK
Children of a Lesser God

The play, *Children of a Lesser God*, details the romance and marriage of a spirited deaf woman and a speech teacher whom she meets at a school for the deaf. Although she lives in a deaf world, she refuses to learn to speak, believing that instead, the hearing world should learn to sign.

RENÉ MILOT
Screaming Rabbit

Criss Angel (illusionist of the TV show *Mind-freak*), with Cirque du Soleil, created a joined venture entitled: "Believe" in Las Vegas at the Luxor Hotel. This image is the final illustration of a lenticular panel. It depicts "Lucky," Criss Angel's stage rabbit, as part of eight-foot-tall framed paintings set in a room—a hall of portraits for the public to get a taste of the act as they proceed toward the stage. Because of the nature of Criss Angel's illusions, a goth/surreal/grunge mood, with a sense of the unknown, had to be created. Working with a great art director, the struggle was mainly with the technical aspect of digitally creating an eight-foot-tall image that was striking while maintaining the quality of details necessary because of the proximity of the viewer. As an assignment, it was the most challenging deadline I had ever encountered, due to the production demands; I was fortunate to work with a great creative team.

ALEX MURAWSKI
Mavis

Mavis Staples's singing voice is a force of nature, and since the 1960s has set the musical tone for the civil rights movement. Her latest album, *We'll Never Turn Back*, continued in that inspirational vein, as did her headlining performance at The Blind Willie McTell Blues Festival. I saw this poster as a chance to pay tribute to her spirit and create an image that evokes the power of that time, of good literally rising from the ashes.

ROBERT NEUBECKER
Ann Landers

I'm not a portrait artist per se, so I focused on her most recognizable feature—her hair. I did endless funny big hair sketches. We settled on a type treatment using all of the groundbreaking topics that she covered in her column. She was the first person ever to print the word "homosexual" in a major newspaper, for instance, and came out early against the Vietnam War. Her real name was Eppie Lederer and she was a truly remarkable woman. This image takes its inspiration from a Push Pin era, Milton Glazer cover of a Philip Roth novel in which he used type in place of eyes.

Tim O'Brien

Scrum

In the middle of a hot summer, a trio of rugby billboards came in and consumed many weeks. Minimal reference was available and I was to paint three works that showed some brushwork and looked like classic paintings. Taking them on one at a time, I was working through the assignment. This was a difficult one—a scrum of players all knotted in battle. My agent was anxious for me but I kept telling him that the art director, Kevin O'Shea, was great and his comments made the art better each time. Before painting, I could tell this one was special. I love that it got into the show and was well received. Cheers to Kevin and my agent, Peter Lott, for making it easy.

ISTVAN OROSZ
Darwin

Posters are my passion. I love working on them, especially Escher-like images. This was another great opportunity to work with SpotCo on a poster for The New York Botanical Gardens.

Zachariah O'Hora

The Ultimate Food Fight!
This is a poster I designed for the 4th Annual Vendy Awards. It's a contest that pits the best New York City street food vendors against each other in a cook-off. I was inspired by Japanese monster flick posters and Mexican showdown wrestling posters.

Zachariah O'Hora

Speaking Truth to Power
This is a poster I designed for the annual NYC Grassroots Media Conference. This year's theme was about speaking truth to power: finding ways to drown out the official talking heads and give people with alternate or seldom-heard viewpoints a chance to be heard.

MICHAEL PARASKEVAS

Hampton Classic 2008

The Hampton Classic is one of the finest-run shows in the United States for show jumping. I've been privileged to have been selected from a long list of entries for this poster four times in the last 20 years. The horse world has always been attractive to me as an artist. I've drawn endless sketchbooks from this event over the years. This year's poster was inspired by on-the-spot sketches I did the previous year while walking the show grounds. I worked in acrylic and watercolor on white paper, without sketching in pencil. I always just work it with the brush.

MICHAEL PARASKEVAS
Hampton Classic 2008 Ticket

This painting of the Grand Prix Sunday crowd at the Hampton Classic Horse show was originally my choice for the poster for that event. But they picked another painting. I was happy they did use this for the ticket stub for the final day, Grand Prix Sunday. Working from photos and sketches, the final painting is acrylic and watercolor on illustration board. And believe me, these people really look like this.

VALERIA PETRONE

Carry Your Bag For You
The campaign was to promote the service of delivering the luggage without lugging. I was free to interpret the concept.

RED NOSE STUDIO
Smell Opportunity
Created for advertising the *Directory of Illustration*, the topic of smelling opportunity seemed perfect for grafting a dog's nose onto a man's face. Thanks to art director David Plunkert for sharing that vision with me.

EDEL RODRIGUEZ
Ring Around the Moon
This painting was used as the poster promoting a performance of *Ring Around the Moon* at Soulpepper Theatre in Toronto. The play is set in a 1940s French chateau, and places the main character in the middle of a love triangle involving herself and a set of twins.

ICON
Poster for ICON5, the illustration conference in New York City. The image was used on all collateral material and as banners hanging on street lamps around Manhattan.

EDEL RODRIGUEZ

A Raisin in the Sun
This painting was used as the poster promoting a performance of *A Raisin in the Sun* at Soulpepper Theatre in Toronto. The story is about the plight of a black family in Chicago's Southside in the 1950s.

EDEL RODRIGUEZ

MTV Ad
This was a magazine ad for MTVTres, the Spanish language television
music network

Yuko Shimizu
AIDS Girl

JUNICHI TSUNEOKA

Citizen Cope Poster

My approach to this poster was to create a character that I could associate with the name "citizen cope." I came up with the character based on typical '50s "good citizen" images. Since it was an acoustic concert, I also created a frog character with the speakers turned off. Then I put these pieces together to create its own world. I like coming up with character illustration. That way I can put a lot of personality into it and that seems to communicate the subject well.

MARK STUTZMAN
Rigoletto

The opera *Rigoletto* tragically portrays a sharp-tongued, cursed court jester's entanglement in social hierarchy. The illustration depicts Rigoletto at a pivotal point, grieving over his daughter's murder, which was brought on by his corrupt ways. The high point of view, angled, contrasting floor pattern, and monochromatic scheme are all intended to add tension and focus to Rigoletto. His posture is pathetic and weak while his jester's baton smiles and mocks his pain. There were several attempts at his costume colors until all agreed that red was the most dramatic and symbolic.

MARK STUTZMAN

Norma

The opera *Norma* depicts a druidess who threatens to sacrifice her children in order to punish an unfaithful for his infidelity. Gallic calligraphy spawned the inspiration for the illustration. The main character becomes part of a design that symbolically represents the Druid lifestyle. This is not the only Norma I did. My first depiction was a more mature woman, but the client decided she should be younger and prettier. Although a printing risk, metallic gold paint was used on the illustration to add to the Old-World feel. Of course, a successful test scan was done prior to taking that plunge.

POL TURGEON

Post Card

These illustrations have been used as promotional postcards for the *Threshold of the Eye* exhibition presented at the Museum of American Illustration at the Society of Illustrators. Two images were needed—one that would represent the commissioned work, and one for the personal work—both in a graphic environment that would link them together.

POL TURGEON

Pinocchio

How to come up with a version of Pinocchio that would make him new, unique, yet—well—Pinocchio-esk? Maybe a circus musical based around the character? Yes, a circus musical! That got me looking in a direction that I would not have otherwise.

BRUCE WALDMAN
Giant

The assignment for this illustration was to create the image of a giant in the process of kneeling down, or rising up—the interpretation of which of these actions was taking place is left to the discretion of the viewer. Christine Morrison gave me excellent suggestions for the image, and then gave me the freedom to develop the illustration in accordance with my own creative instincts and vision. I tried to create a dynamic graphic composition by forcing the viewer's eye up against the edge of the page, and then stopping it with a vertical red strip to cause a kind of visual tension. This piece is a monoprint.

SAM WEBER
Guardsman

226 ADVERTISING

SAM WEBER
Glengarry Glenross

SAM WEBER
Parfumerie

Kyle T. Webster

One Flew Over the Cuckoo's Nest

Since its opening, Triad Stage has used illustration for its promotional materials for every single production. After several years spent admiring the theater's top notch posters, I was delighted to get a call from Troy Tyner at Mitre to do three(!) posters for the 2008 season. Of the three I produced, this piece for *One Flew Over the Cuckoo's Nest* was my favorite image and I am honored that it was accepted into the Society's annual this year.

NATE WILLIAMS

Soulville

I illustrated for the cover of *Soulville*, a collection of kid-friendly songs by the genre's giants backed by a kids' chorus. The colorful liner notes provide an introduction to soul music, with notes about the songs and original recording artists, plus fun poems that point to the importance of this genre in American history. The album made many "Best of 2008" lists, including *USA Today*'s and NPR's. This is my second cover for independent label, Little Monster Records.

NATE WILLIAMS
Sherlock Holmes

I created this silk-screened image as part of a six-artist series curated by Tristan Rault and printed by Luciano Muruato. They were sold at the Museo de Arte Latinoamericano de Buenos Aires (MALBA).

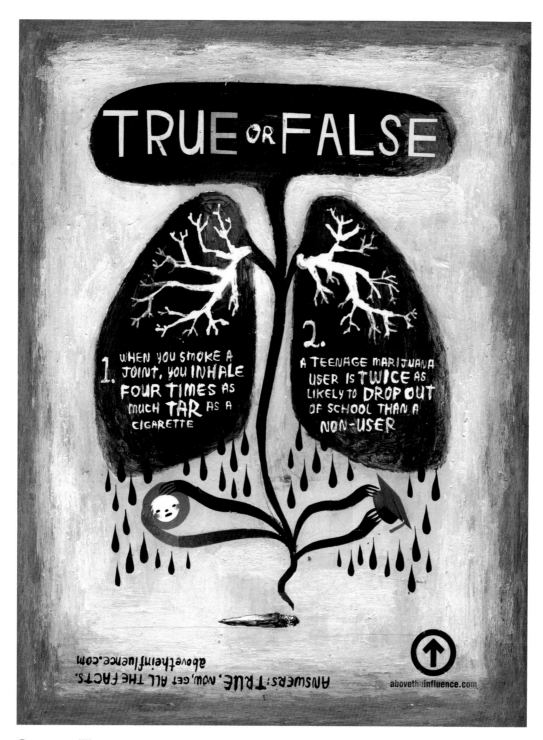

GORDON WIEBE

True or False

This is one of three illustrations done with Lowe New York for the National Youth Anti-Drug Media Campaign, "Above the Influence." Each of the three posters features a true or false statement, revealing certain facts about marijuana use. The campaign's goal is to help teens stay "above the influence" by making them aware of the influences around them and preparing them to stand up to the pressures that might motivate them to use drugs.

CRAIG ZUCKERMAN
Funk-Eyeman

This illustration, commissioned by Gabriel Mattar at DDB Berlin, was an adaptation of the Las Vegas line, "What happens in Vegas, stays in Vegas!" He wanted to show a Hieronymus Bosch type of scene, with little vignettes of people, animals, elves, imaginary figures, etc. This way, each time the art is viewed we may see more things. Well, the elves and imaginary figures did not make the final cut. Although the concept was his, he did allow me to contribute how each image, or scene would be portrayed. So, regardless of how one lives one's life, "Funk" sunglasses will shield the world from your bloodshot eyes!

TAKASHI AKIYAMA

Jishin-Earthquake Japan (Namazu)
This earthquake poster has enshrined namazue, the catfish, which has been a god of the earthquake in Japan since the Edo period. And the earthquake hell of Japan is a fire. The namazue was drawn.

TAKASHI AKIYAMA

Jishin-Earthquake Japan (Shinkansen)
Fear of the Shinkansen being derailed was imagined in this *Jishin-Earthquake Japan* poster.

SCOTT BAKAL
Intergalactic Neighbors #1

JUSTINE BECKETT
Biodegradable
Promotional calendar image illustrating the importance of using biodegradable products.

MARK BENDER
Snow Globe
Promises Magazine, for Pittsburgh Children's Hospital, commissioned
me to create an illustration for an article called "Safe Keeping." The article
dealt with protecting your children in the winter. Director Ellen Maso and
Designer Susan Limoncelli always give me complete freedom and the
opportunity to push concepts.

LAUREN SIMKIN BERKE
Mary Lou Chapman 1

MARC BURCKHARDT

Babe Ruth

When Faith Rittenberg at MLB asked me to do a portrait of Babe Ruth, I was excited, but when she told me it was for the very last All Star game to be played in Yankee Stadium, I have to admit I got a little nervous. The pressure! In the end, I think we knocked it out of the ballpark.

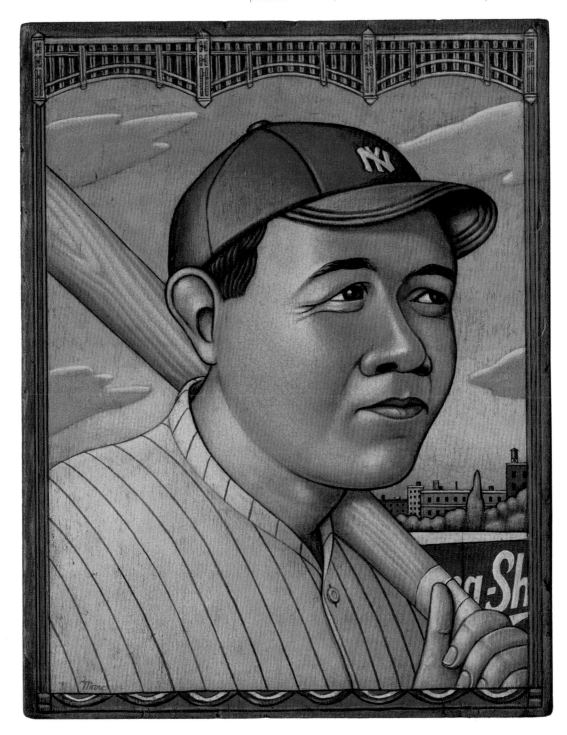

CHRIS BUZELLI

Pre-teen Anxiety

This painting was for an article about pre-teen anxiety. Every so often I take a slight turn from my normal painting path in hopes of a surprise. Usually, I make a sketch, blow it up, refine the sketch, and then cover it all up with oil paint. I always miss the soft edges, thumb smudges, and free mark making of the drawing. Lately, I've been trying to incorporate more graphite drawing into my final paintings, as I did with this piece.

ROBERT CASILLA
Nose in Book

PETER CHAN
The Gift

Film director Hayao Miyazaki (*My Neighbor Totoro*) has been trying to protect the Totoro Sayama Forest from urban sprawl. A group of Bay Area artists formed an organization called the Totoro Forest Project. The group asked the animation community to donate original art for an auction fundraiser to support Miyazaki's efforts. All participating artists responded to the same assignment question: "What is your Totoro?" For me, the image reflects our industrial world being greedy and blind. Yet there is a glimmer of hope in the puppet man's gift to the child. A gift of comfort, innocence, and purity.

JOSH COCHRAN
Greenwich Village
Catalogue cover for The New School. The drawing had to depict the interior of a classroom as well as the surrounding Greenwich Village.

TIMOTHY COOK

Roots Music

This representation of traditional American music was created for the 2008 National Public Radio calendar. I wanted the illustration to have an old-time spirit like a lot of the music I listen to on public stations. A childhood memory inspired the overall feeling. As a boy, I accompanied my father to the television station where he preached sermons on the air. The subsequent broadcast featured live bluegrass. The power and clarity of the sound, as well as the heartfelt emotions, moved me. The instruments resonated a type of siren song that seemed to reel me into a different, earlier time.

KATHERINE DUNN
Animal Friends

This piece is a montage of some of the many animal portraits I've been hired to do. Now I publish this piece as an archival print, with monies from each sale being donated to animal organizations that help senior animals in need. My goal with any animal portrait is to provide a conduit for the owners to feel the heart and soul of their animal companions, a comfort for them after their pet is gone. I work traditionally with acrylic, pastel, and pencil and then I often layer drawings into the piece.

LEO ESPINOSA
Recollect Dead Custom Vans Show (shoes)
A printed piece and a custom pair of Vans sneakers were featured in a group show at Cave Gallery in Detroit. The show loosely blended the spirit of Halloween and traditions of Day of the Dead with sneaker and snowboard culture.

BART J. FORBES
Beets

CHRIS GALL

Harvesting Natural Gas
This art was created for a company that promotes compressed natural gas as a clean and safe alternative fuel. The key idea was that it could be cultivated in many unexpected areas of the country and in some ways resemble farming.

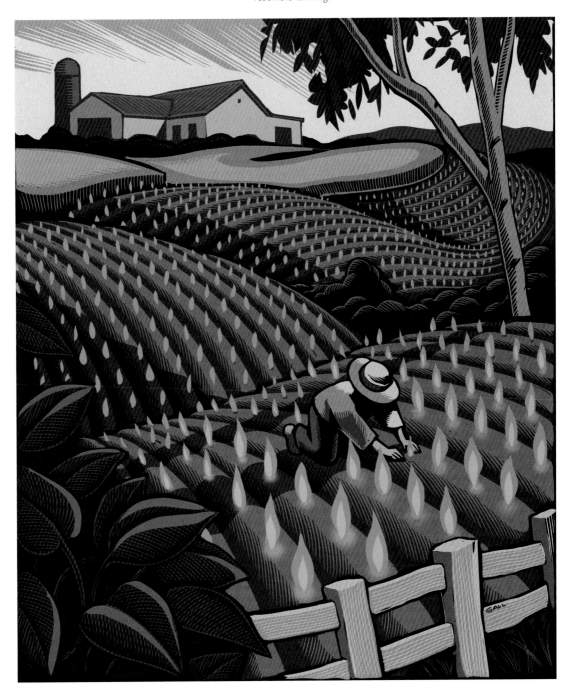

RICHARD A. GOLDBERG

Bon Voyage
The empty nest is sometimes facilitated by a gentle nudge from the powers that be.

LUIS GRANE
They Are Waiting

JESSIE HARTLAND
Tribeca Graphic

A painting of my neighborhood in downtown New York City, which has been reproduced and is sold as limited-edition prints at a local shop. The painting features well-known spots: the trapeze school, the park with a playground, favorite restaurants and bakeries, and is primarily purchased for children's rooms.

TIM HEITZ
The Hill

I was extremely honored when a coworker of mine invited me to be a part of The Totoro Forest Project. The purpose of the project was to raise funds for the beloved Totoro Forest in Japan, the inspiration of Hayao Miyazaki's animated classic, *My Neighbor Totoro*. Each artist involved was to create their own version of the Totoro—a creature or spirit that only children can see. In my piece, the nature that surrounds the children comes to life and takes form. It acts as their friend, their protector, and their companion, watching over them wherever they go.

JODY HEWGILL
The Secret Fall of Constance Wilde
This was a fairly quick assignment. The concept of the two floating heads was given to me by the art director, whereas I usually prefer to read the play and present my own concepts. Some artistic license was applied here because the reference photos of Constance Wilde were quite blurry and small.

JODY HEWGILL

Legacy of Light

Theatre poster for the Arena Stage world premiere of *Legacy of Light*, a play about two women physicists who lead parallel lives and struggle with their inner conflict between work and maternal desire. One woman is Emilie du Châtelet, an actual 18th century physicist, and the other is a fictitious contemporary physicist. Originally, I had a small fetus in the center of the nebula (within Emilie's dress), but unfortunately I was asked to take it out.

BRAD HOLLAND
Beached

BRAD HOLLAND
Magic Catch

JORDIN ISIP
Dead Metaphor

This was created for "Lost Youth Found," Virgin Mobile USA's Regeneration Gallery and Benefit Auction. Curator Rich Jacobs invited twenty artists to make a piece on the supplied 24 by 24 inch wood panel.

Proceeds from the sales of the artwork went directly to support the organizations working on the issues of youth homelessness. The mixed-media image was created with that subject matter in mind.

FRANCES JETTER

Locked Tongue

The "Art of Democracy" built a network of exhibitions and events that took place nationwide in the fall of 2008. New York, San Francisco, Chicago, Seattle, Atlanta, Puerto Rico, Muncie, and other locations created powerful exhibitions at a critical time in American democracy. I designed the logo, which was commissioned by Stephen Fredericks and Art Hazelwood, who jointly started the "Art of Democracy." Stephen Fredericks asked me to do the poster, based on the logo, for the New York Society of Etcher's exhibition at The National Arts Club.

GWENDA KACZOR
New York City, Real or Imagined
This piece was created for a collaborative book project which was art directed by Julia Breckenreid and shown at ICON5. Illustrators were asked to create an illustration based on their own personal perspective of New York City. I felt the concept of the yellow brick road represented well my own experience of trying to balance the realities of living in the city with the idea of following one's dreams.

SOOSA KIM
Sweet & Honey

ROMAN KLONEK

Ancient Forest

All members of Sturges Reps do a piece for a calendar every year. The topic for 2009 was "going green." I chose the "ancient forest" because immediately I had a hurly-burly but rough picture in my head. I sketched a bunch of exotic plants and strange animals and mixed them in a well-adjusted composition. In the end I did some masks in Photoshop and filled them up with woodcut texture.

MARIA EUGENIA LONGO
Casal

WILLIAM LOW
Greeting the Dawn

ROBERT MACKENZIE
Union Square

BILL MAYER

The Max Awards

An obvious direction was to use the inner workings of the brain in a kind of tenth grade science experiment with beakers, gears, belts, and horns in a kind of surreal Rube Goldberg drawing. Only I am too lazy and inept to make the damn thing work the way he did.

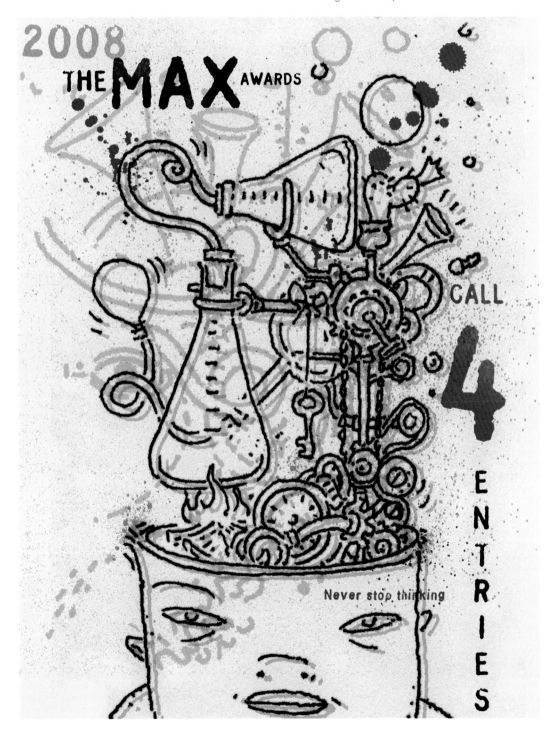

Adam McCauley

Social Security Resources Further Reading

This was one of a series of about twenty illustrations for a publication published by The Center for Retirement at Boston College. The brochure explains how best to claim your benefits when you decide to retire. The challenge was to find iconography that could work through- out as a series; in this case I used the circle/dot to represent units of money, units of time, paths of direction, etc. This particular piece was about finding further resources and publications to help with these key decisions.

YAN NASCIMBENE
MTA Poster

KEN ORVIDAS
Global Vision

Agnes Scott College is a liberal arts women's college in Georgia. The ASC President's Report is a strategic plan of signature initiatives. It's intended to enhance the Agnes Scott experience for future generations by engaging a wider world, forging new connections with people, institutions, and ideas on campus, around their region, and across the globe. The young woman on the cover of the report is all about engaging a wider world.

VALERIA PETRONE
Catalogue Cover
Commissioned piece for the cover and interior illustrations of a catalogue for kids book publisher Feltrinelli, to be printed on the occasion of the Bologna's Book Fair. The logo of the kids is a black cat so I created this character. The same image was used to build the publisher booth at the book fair.

EMMANUEL PIERRE
One Thousand and One Accessories

Marc Rosenthal
Student Loans

Chris Sheban

Duluth Reindeer

We made the nose green so as not to infringe on any "Rudolph" copyright issues. I kept lighting matches, blowing them out, and photographing the smoke. After about 300 attempts and setting off the smoke detector, I had my reference. Reindeer wouldn't cooperate either.

WHITNEY SHERMAN

Treedo

Treedo was created for the Urban Forest Project/Baltimore. The banners were designed to raise awareness of environmental issues. The project has been done in many major cities across the U.S. My piece took into consideration the topic and location paying homage to John Waters' nickname for Baltimore: the Hairdo Capital of the World. The strong vertical shape of the banner dictated much of the way this piece looks. The banners were later recycled into one-of-a-kind tote bags. You saw the Treedo Tote if you made it to the exhibition.

MICHAEL SLOAN

NYC Outward Bound Benefit Invitation 2008
I've been creating the cover illustration for NYCOB's annual benefit invitations for 12 years, and I continue to be challenged by the substantial text requirements, which convey the organization's mission and must be integrated into the illustration. I found inspiration for this cover in some antique carnival posters. My design included a circular window in the center: the scene of the children and school printed on the inside of the back cover.

DAVE STOLTE
Bacon Surprise

Illustrator Dave Stolte studied Studio Art at California State University Long Beach, then spent twenty-five years in the world of design doing other people's work before finding his own voice. (Sometimes these things take a while.) Drawing on a history of physical mixed-media collage and useless Post-it doodles, his images are created using a library of paper textures, found ephemera, and photography, then digitally composed under his original pencil sketches. *Bacon Surprise* was commissioned by Fraülein Affair Gallery in Costa Mesa, California, for its opening show "Love for Breakfast," and found its way into *Illustrators 51* via blatant pandering to the irresistible combination of bacon and sex.

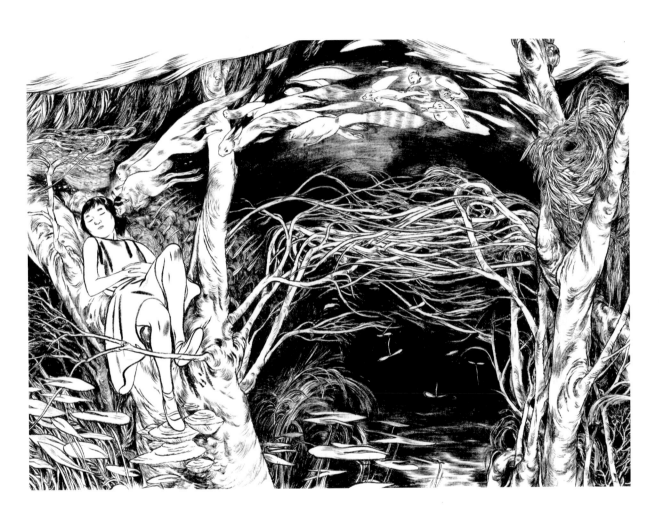

JILLIAN TAMAKI
Totoro Forest

WALTER VASCONCELOS

Black Mail

This illustration was made for a promotional calendar. Its designers gave me only one word: "blackmail." I made some little sketches and went to the computer. The image of the Devil immediately emerged as a symbol of people who write unsigned letters. The technique is mixed and, as always, there are dozens and dozens of layers finished in Photoshop. I really enjoyed doing this work.

NATE WILLIAMS

Animals in Trees
I was commissioned by Urban Outfitters stores to create custom artwork for two pillows for their Fall/Winter 2008 Artist Series home collection. This special collection is made up of art from a hand-selected group of rising art and illustration stars. The line also includes framed prints, one of which reproduces my artwork.

JULIA WOOLF
Untitled

This piece was done for The Totoro Forest Project, which was put together to help raise money to save the Sayama Forest outside of Tokyo. This forest was the inspiration for the fantastic animated film, *My Neighbor Totoro*, made by Hayao Miyazaki. I was invited to take part in this fundraising exhibition/auction along with 200 other artists. We were all asked to create an original work of art inspired by the film. I was very pleased to be asked to join this project, as *Totoro* is probably my favorite animated film. It was not hard to be inspired. When illustrating I always start with a very rough sketch and then I scan that into the computer and work digitally in Photoshop. It was a fun project to do.

BOOK

ISABELLE DERVAUX
ILLUSTRATOR

A native of France, Isabelle received her art education at the University of Lille. Soon after completing her studies, she made her way to New York where she developed a client list filled with the most well known names in advertising, retail, publishing and entertainment. She has worked extensively in the United States, Japan, and Europe for such clients as *The New Yorker*, Barneys New York, British Airways, Parco, and many others. She has received recognition from *American Illustration*, *Communication Arts*, *Print*, and the Society of Publication Designers. Her work is also part of MoMA's permanent collection and she has had several exhibitions of her work in Tokyo. Isabelle has taught Illustration at CCA and Parsons The New School of Design, and now lives with her husband and two children in Manhattan.

LES KANTUREK
ILLUSTRATOR, DESIGNER

Les Kanturek is a book designer, illustrator, and, since 1991, a teacher in the illustration department at Parsons The New School for Design. His work, as both illustrator and designer, has appeared in *3x3*, *American Illustration*, the Society of Illustrators of LA, *Print's Regional Design Annual*, and *Print Casebook Best Covers*. In addition, Les's books and covers have been recognized by Book Builders of Boston, VOYA (Voice of Youth Advocates) Annual Nonfiction Honor List, and The Society of School Librarians International. Les divides his time between Long Island and Manhattan, and usually works under the watchful eye of something or someone mounted on his studio wall. He is presently working on a visual narrative on the death of Ernest Hemingway.

JAMES MCMULLAN
ILLUSTRATOR

Four highlights from James McMullan's long and varied career are the paintings he made of a Brooklyn disco, which became the visual inspiration for the movie *Saturday Night Fever*; the animated film, *Dec 25th, 1914*, created for PBS Television; the 65-foot-long mural he designed for the Mitzi Newhouse Theater; and the award-winning *I Stink!*, which went on to achieve picture-book glory. The 70 posters he has designed as Principal Poster Artist of Lincoln Center Theater are being celebrated in 2010 with an exhibition at the Lincoln Center Library of the Performing Arts. He is the author of three books: *Revealing Illustrations*, *The Theater Posters of James McMullan*, and *High-Focus Drawing*, based on his teaching at the School of Visual Arts. A 192-page book of poems, selected by Julie Andrews and Illustrated by the artist, was published in the fall of 2009.

SEMADAR MEGGED
PHILOMEL BOOKS

Semadar Megged has designed children's books for Dutton, Bantam Doubleday Dell, and Putnam, and is now in the combined role of art director and designer at Philomel, working exclusively on editor Patricia Gauch's books. When Semadar wants to work the other side of her brain she switches to adult books, designing covers for New Directions.

WENDELL MINOR
ILLUSTRATOR

Wendell Minor is the award-winning illustrator of over 40 picture books for children, among them many classics by Newbery award-winning author Jean Craighead George, including the 2008 release of *The Wolves are Back*. His works also include the illustrations for Robert Burleigh's *Abraham Lincoln Comes Home* and illustrations for Buzz Aldrin's *Reaching For the Moon*, a *New York Times* Bestseller and *Publishers Weekly* Best Books of the Year 2005. *If You Were a Penguin*, written by his wife Florence, is Pennsylvania's 2009 selection for their "One Book, Every Young Child" program, and *Look to the Stars*, Wendell's second collaboration with astronaut and moon-walker Buzz Aldrin, will be published in May 2009.

ROBERT ANDREW PARKER
ILLUSTRATOR

Robert Andrew Parker's illustrations have appeared in *The New Yorker*, *The New York Times*, *Fortune*, *Time*, and *Sports Illustrated*, among many other publications. Numerous books include, most recently, words and pictures for *Piano Starts Here*, a children's book about Art Tatum. Robert's work is held in the collections of MoMA, the Metropolitan Museum of Art, the Whitney Museum, the Brooklyn Museum of Art, the Morgan Library, and others. He illustrated the poetry for the 1966 film *The Days of Wilfred Owen*, narrated by Richard Burton, and created drawings and painting for the MGM 1955 film *Lust for Life*. He taught at the School of Visual Arts from 1960-70; Parsons School of Design from 1980-92; and Gerit Rietveld Academy, Amsterdam, in 1985; and was a Guggenheim Fellow, 1969-70. His work has been exhibited at Davis & Langdale in New York City, and he lives in West Cornwall, Connecticut.

SERGIO RUZZIER
ILLUSTRATOR

Sergio Ruzzier was born in Milan, Italy, in 1966, and moved to New York City in 1995. His artistic education comes from years of visiting museums and medieval churches in Northern and Central Italy, and from working in libraries and antique bookstores. In 1989 he created a series of comic strips for *Linus*, and later gave birth to "Bruno" for *Lupo Alberto Magazine*.

The Room of Wonders (FSG, 2006) and *Amandina* (Roaring Brook, 2008) are among his picture books. *Hey Rabbit!* will be published by Roaring Brook in 2010. His work has been awarded by *American Illustration*, The Society of Illustrators, and *Communication Arts*. Sergio won the Parents' Choice Gold Medal for *The Room of Wonders* and for his illustrations in *Why Mole Shouted* (FSG, 2004).

DAVID SANDLIN
ILLUSTRATOR

David Sandlin was born in Belfast, Northern Ireland, in 1956, and has lived in New York City since 1980. He recently completed volume seven of *A Sinner's Progress*, a series of narrative artists' books that range from hand-silkscreened editions to a Fantagraphic-printed pulp-style comic. He teaches at the School of Visual Arts and publishes his work whenever and wherever he's asked, including in *The New York Times*, *The New Yorker*, *Newsweek*, *Time*, *Spin*, *The Walrus*, and *Harper's*. He also publishes comics and graphic narratives in *Hotwire*, *BLAB!*, and *The Ganzfeld*.

LAURA STUTZMAN
ILLUSTRATOR

Laura Stutzman attended the Art Institute of Pittsburgh and began her career as an illustrator with *The Pittsburgh Press*, followed by a move to Washington, DC, working in advertising as an illustrator and designer. In 1984 she co-founded Eloqui, a studio devoted exclusively to illustration, with her husband Mark Stutzman. Her clients have included PBS, MCI, CBS, Simon & Schuster, *National Geographic*, Sleeping Bear Press, the U.S. Postal Service, Zippo, and Time/Life Books.

SAM WEBER
ILLUSTRATOR

Born in Alaska, Sam Weber grew up in Deep River, Ontario, Canada. After attending the Alberta College of Art and Design in Calgary, he moved to New York to pursue illustration and attend graduate school at the School of Visual Arts. His studio is in Brooklyn.

The Immaterial Time
It's a story about a boy. His youth in Sicily. The years when terrorism was at its height in Italy, the *brigate rosse* (red brigade) in the background. He and his friend start to copy the terrorists' behavior and kidnap a young girl.

GOLD MEDAL WINNER
ADAM McCAULEY

The Monsterologist Endpaper Stamps
The concept of these stamps was born from the challenge of bridging the first few spreads in *The Monsterologist*, this crazy picture/gift book project. The setup here is that Dracula has sent the retired scientist a letter. I wanted a way to arc into the book, so I thought the endpapers would look great as sheets of stamps. The title page is the unopened envelope, and a couple more spreads in is the Count's opened letter. The book was made to look like a collection of the Monsterologist's journal files and sketchbooks—his lifetime of work and his interviews with all kinds of monsters.

Bullet Rogan
One of the earlier paintings from *We Are the Ship: The Story of Negro League Baseball*, this painting is one of my favorites. I love drawing and painting hands and feet so I tend to make them a bit larger than they really should be. Rogan was a rather small man, but had a very big presence and could throw the ball just as hard as the best of them. I particularly like the darkness of his skin set against his white uniform and the green bench he is sitting on. It reminds me of my Little League days. (Not to say that I sat the bench because, if memory serves me, I wasn't too shabby a player, if I do say so myself).

Things Fall Apart
This is the first of ten covers I was asked to create for a series of novels by the African author Chinua Achebe. This book is titled Things Fall Apart and deals with the clash of cultures and the destruction of African village life with the arrival of European missionaries. I submitted a number of ideas to Helen Yentus, the art director, and this image seemed to say it all in a simple manner.

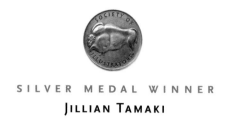

Half World
This is a wrap-around cover for the young adult novel *Half World* by Canadian author Hiromi Goto. In the story, 14-year-old Melanie is forced to enter a dark dimension between the living and the dead in order to rescue her parents. The book also contains a dozen black-and-white interior illustrations.

STEVE ADAMS
Rest

[redacted]

SARAH ATLEE
Normal, OK: Hinton Geary
Hinton Geary is from Normal, OK, a community of fictional characters suggested by place names in and around Oklahoma. I wrote, illustrated, and self-published the book *Normal, OK*, which is available in paperback at Lulu.com or in limited edition hardcover (signed and numbered by the artist) at sarahatlee.com. The original art from *Normal* was part of the first Art 365 exhibit created by the Oklahoma Visual Arts Coalition. Hinton Geary is a retired English teacher. He believes he is the host vessel for a super-intelligent alien visitor. He wears bow ties.

ANNA AND ELENA BALBUSSO

Bath

This is the first of three illustrations from the classic children's picture book *Les Cygnes Sauvages (The Wild Swans)* by Hans Christian Andersen (Odense 1805–Denmark 1875). This famous classic tale tells the story of a young girl, Princess Elisa, and her search for her lost 11 brothers. After their mother's death, the new Queen became angry and put a wicked curse on the kingdom that transformed the 11 boys into swans. In *Bath*, the bad Queen throws three toads in Eliza's bath, but Elisa is so good and so innocent that evil magic cannot harm her. To transmit the atmosphere of the fairy tale, we looked to Symbolist painters such as Caspar David Friedrich, John Henry Fuseli, and Gustave Moreau. This movement helped us to communicate the sensations of spirituality, imagination, and dreams. We wished to create the mysterious atmosphere through nature, landscape, color, and the contrast of light and shadow. We preferred a style not overly realistic and detailed. We use mixed media: acrylic and digital. Our visible brush strokes are not digital but are handmade. First we use acrylic on paper and then Photoshop.

ANNA AND ELENA BALBUSSO

Fly

This is the second of three illustrations from *Les Cygnes Sauvages (The Wild Swans)*. *Fly* represents the metamorphosis: Elisa sees 11 wild swans flying. At the moment when the sun finally sinks below the horizon, the swans turn into 11 handsome princes, Elisa's brothers.

ANNA AND ELENA BALBUSSO
Rock

This is the third of three illustrations from *Les Cygnes Sauvages (The Wild Swans)*. In *Rock*, Elisa and her brothers are on a rock. Dark clouds on the horizon warn of a coming storm.

Anna and Elena Balbusso
Wife

This is the first of two illustrations from the classic novel *The Age of Innocence* by Edith Wharton. The story is set in upper-class New York City in the 1870s. This was a rather small group of families and everybody gossiped about everybody else. Newland and May are about to marry. Then May's cousin, Ellen, arrives from Europe and Newland Archer falls in love with her. The images are connected between them. A man with two women—his wife and his lover. In *Wife*, Newland is reading a book in the library. He is thinking about his boring wife: she never surprises him with a new idea or emotion. In this image it is very important to communicate the psychology of the characters—their private passions and the contrast between their emotions. We have chosen an impressionist interpretation with a style not overly realistic and detailed, using visible brush strokes, hard contrast between light and shadow, and intense warm colors. Our references were the French and Italian art movements of the late 1800s—the Impressionist and the Macchiaioli. We use mixed media: acrylic and digital. Our brush strokes are not digital but are handmade. First we use acrylic on paper and then Photoshop.

ANNA AND ELENA BALBUSSO
Kiss

This is the second of two illustrations from *The Age of Innocence*. In *Kiss*, Newland meets his lover. He falls to his knees on the floor and kisses the Countess Olenska's shoe.

ANGELA BARBALACE
The White Coat

The finished painting provides the conceptual idea of characters depicted from all walks of life, such as the white collar worker to the unemployed. I refined the piece in a series of sketches until I was satisfied with a sense of personality and perspective. You can see how perspective plays an important part throughout all my work, especially in my street scenes. The rainy setting brings a sense of originality and also gives me the opportunity to show my artistic skill.

SERGE BLOCH
Mon Petit Roi

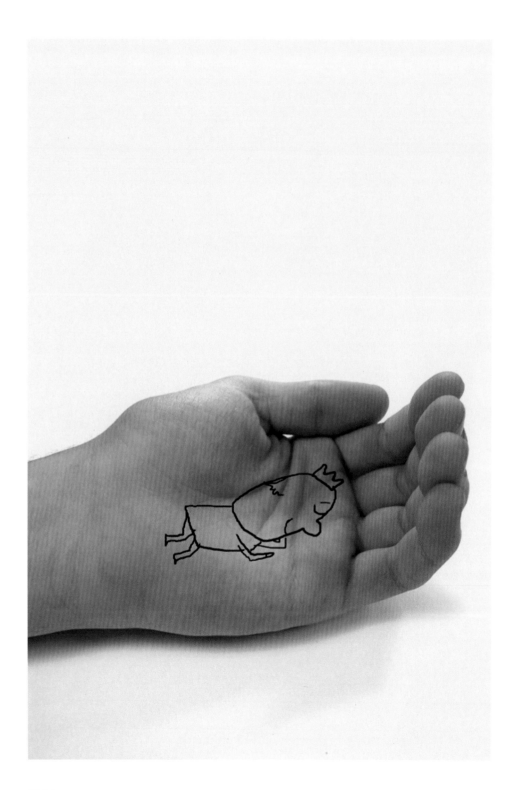

the ENEMY

a book
about
peace

DAVIDE CALI
and SERGE BLOCH

MARC BURCKHARDT

Von Dutch Portrait 1

These two portraits are of the same man: Kenny Howard, otherwise known as Von Dutch, the infamous artist, pin-striper, mechanic, knife-maker, and eccentric. They're bookends of a sort, showing Howard in his army years as his artistic identity was just emerging, and years later, when his demons began to consume him.

PAUL BUCKLEY
The World According to Garp

PAUL BUCKLEY
Of Mice and Men

LOU BROOKS

The Dead Travel Fast

I wanted the image to evoke a gasp, a mood of hair-raising unexpected shock. Just the book's title alone, *The Dead Travel Fast*, convinced me that if a vampire ever shows up, it will be quietly, in the middle of the night, in the dark—a grinning thirsty guy at the foot of my bed, or star-ing through a rain-streaked bedroom window. To get myself started on the assignment, I watched *Dracula's Daughter* (my favorite vampire movie) several times with the lights out: The drawing is inked onto watercolor paper, and then brought into Photoshop for coloring.

JIM BURKE
Bartholdi's Studio: Creating Liberty

CHRIS BUZELLI
The Last Synapsid

This painting was commissioned by Delacorte Press for Young Readers for *The Last Synapsid* cover. At first, the 350-page manuscript was daunting, but I was quickly drawn into the adventure of Rob, Phoebe, and Sid, the time traveling dinosaur. Usually book covers go through many edits but this one was a breeze—only one small change to the initial sketch.

PHILIP CHEANEY
Rabbit Deity of Drunkenness

JOSEPH CIARDIELLO
Elvin Crow
I had the opportunity to work with the great crime novelist Elmore Leonard on an edition of his book *10 Rules for Writing*. This drawing illustrates rule #7: "Use Regional Dialect, Patois, Sparingly" and depicts a character, Elvin Crowe, from the book *Maximum Bob*.

"Roland was working for the EyetaLians down in Miami when a woman shot him, said he broke into her house.

...It was her pulled the trigger, yeah, but was this dink set it up. He knew it was Roland in the house and told the woman it was somebody broke in. 'Cause he didn't have the nerve to do it hisself. Understand?"

ELVIN Crowe
from MAXIMUM BOB

JOSH COCHRAN

Angkor Wat

A chapter in the book *Lost Civilizations*. This one is about the temple, Angkor Wat, in Cambodia. It was found in 1860 by French botanist Henri Mahout. Archeologists don't really know why the temple city was built, but suspect that it might be some sort of funeral monument for a king. People who've visited report a strange feeling of being suspended in space because of all the reflections of the sky in the water.

JOSH COCHRAN
Lincoln Funeral Train
Illustration for the book *Haunted U.S.A.* This is for a chapter on the Lincoln Funeral Train, which is a ghost train and can sometimes be seen across the United States.

SALLY WERN COMPORT
Last Judgment

I recognized how incomprehensible and horrific The Last Judgment visual could be. So I made the decision, while working with International Bible Society art director Lisa Anderson, to choose a more Disneyesque/Marvelesque version of this apocalyptic event. That this was a project intermittently spanning four years of my professional life helped me develop a sense for the young audience for the publication, which was support material for a South American version of the Bible. I tried to give a sense of the human condition without scaring the wits out of the viewer.

ANDRÉ DA LOBA

Travel

GIANNI DE CONNO
The Pomegranate Seed

Peter de Sève

Standard Hero Behavior
It's always fun to return to the Sword and Sorcery genre of illustration I
loved so much as a young and aspiring illustrator.

JON FOSTER
Lyonesse

ALEXANDRA FRANK

But Oh! That Deep Romantic Chasm Which Slanted

My collages captured first instincts visually. Then I did an enormous amount of reading: *The Arabian Nights*, Greek Mythology, Utopian theory, biographies about Coleridge and what he read: Milton, Shakespeare, *Pilgrim's Progress*, followed by books about the poem: Genghis Khan, laudanum, and dulcimers. For every line after that, I looked up each word in the *OED*. With my initial collage and some other images as inspiration, I painted line by line. Coleridge himself wrote, "Were I a painter I would give outward existence to this, but it will always live in my memory." It was wonderful to give outward existence to his words.

MARK FREDRICKSON

Lydia the Tattooed Lady

The illustration *Lydia the Tattooed Lady* is for a book titled *The Art of the Marx Brothers*. I was given free rein to choose any theme from any of the Marx Brothers movies and illustrate it for the book. *Lydia the Tattooed Lady* has always been my favorite signature Grouch Marx tune from the movie *At the Circus*. Each tattoo depicted on Lydia is mentioned in the song. The tattoo depicting The Wreck of the Hesperus, from the song, is the source of Groucho's concern. If you read Longfellow's poem of the same name, you'll understand why.

DENISE GALLAGHER

Her Guests Considered Her Unconventionally Charming

This work was created as an example of pattern use for Von Glitschka's book *Drip. Dot. Swirl*. The pattern I was assigned reminded me of fragile, tinkling teacups and tiny cakes arranged just so. What would one do, I mused, if while balancing a teacup and thinking of the perfect thing to say, a miniature octopus was spied curled among the cakes and tea? The illustration, created with a very sharp pencil and with digitally added color, pattern, and texture, achieves a balance of mystery and charm one might find in a tea parlor crowded with china and tiny friendly creatures peering out from every corner.

BEPPE GIACOBBE
The Book of Farewells

BEN GIBSON
The Uncles Ten

BEN GIBSON
The Monster Variations

DONATO GIANCOLA
Archer of the Rose

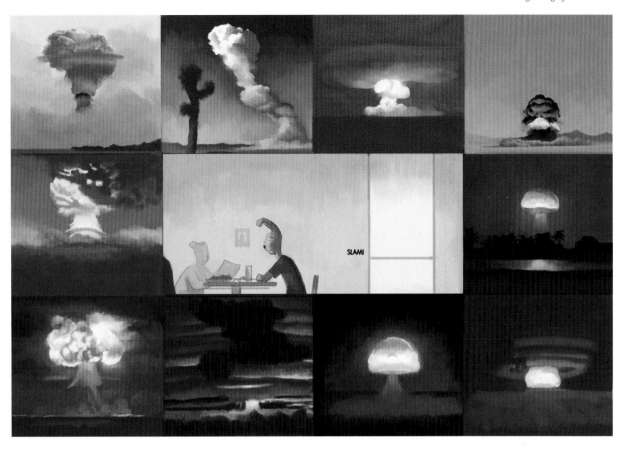

DAVID GORDON
End of the Line

ALESSANDRO GOTTARDO

The City of Thieves
War World II. Colonel Grechko confronts Lev (17-year-old) and Kolya, a Russian army deserter also facing execution. He spares them on the condition that they acquire a dozen eggs for the colonel's daughter's wedding cake.

ALESSANDRO GOTTARDO

Except the Dog
Carlo D'Amicis's book. The questions against the answers, the dogmas against the relativism. All of this conflict became a novel in this book.

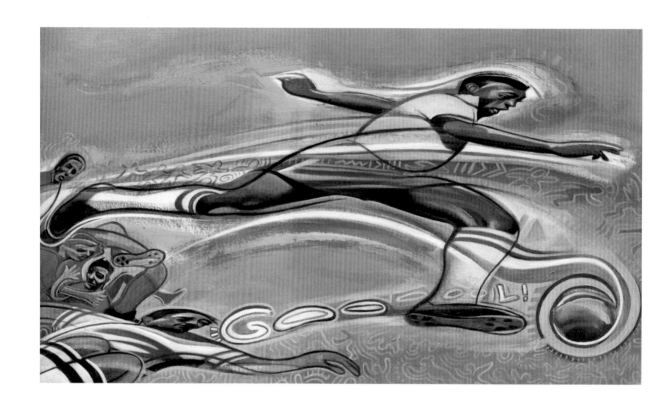

RUDY GUTIERREZ
Pele King of Soccer

GREG HARLIN
We the People

JOHN HENDRIX
Cooking Dirty

The content of this manuscript about a wandering chef's career odyssey—cooking everywhere, from roadside diners to fancy restaurants—seemed like a perfect opportunity to use a rough-edged sketchbook mode of drawing. The goal was to contrast the precise act of cutting, with the chaos of the surrounding scene. The way the drawings were made also needed to reflect that contrast. Thanks to Aaron Artessa for his great direction and confidence.

JODY HEWGILL

Tender Morsels

This young adult novel is a dark fairytale about a woman's escape from the violence and tragedy on earth, to her life in a small forest paradise where she encounters a wild bear-man. The art director, Isabel Warren-Lynch, provided me with a rough sketch of a woman embracing a bear and asked me to develop it further in my own style.

David Ho

The Engine's Child

This illustration was created for the book *The Engine's Child* written by Holly Phillips. The story speaks of a fantasy southeastern/Indian society that is hit by many catastrophic disasters, and a main character who questions her society's faith and values. The publisher wished to see a stone sculpture depicted in the illustration and here's what I came up with.

JEREMY HOLMES

The Green Guide for Horse Owners and Riders
This book offers up detailed information on how to raise and ride horses
in a sustainable manner. Because a major part of the book is dedicated
to teaching one how to properly setup and use the natural resources
surrounding the horse, I figured creating the horse out of those natural
resources felt natural.

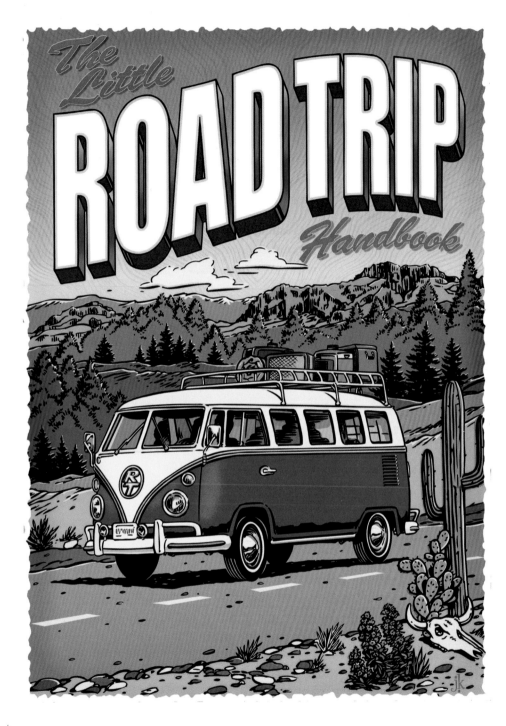

JOHN KACHIK
The Little Road Trip Handbook

This assignment started with a call from Karen Nelson at Sterling Publishing, who gave me my favorite style of art direction. I'm paraphrasing what I recall from that conversation, but it went something like this: "We need an American travel postcard feel with a vintage VW bus driving away in a landscape—you know, do that thing you do." Cool! Other than turning the bus around to see the more interesting side of the vehicle, it developed as she requested. Once a sketch was approved, everything—including the type—was hand drawn to keep a retro feel, then scanned, and colored in Photoshop. As an interesting side note, this is the same kind of bus my family owned for most of my childhood, only ours was green and didn't have a roof rack. Wish I had it today.

JAMES KACZMAN
Lucky Monkey, Unlucky Monkey Cover

AYA KAKEDA
French Baguette Monster

GARY KELLEY
Dark Fiddler

TATSURO KIUCHI
Ya-te-ve-o A Man Eating Tree
This is my piece for the book *BEASTS!*, a collection of beast images by over
90 visual artists curated by Jacob Covey and published by Fantagraphics. I
chose to illustrate Ya-te-veo (a man eating tree). The piece is digitally created with Photoshop with a lot of textures scanned in as layers.

OLIVIER KUGLER
Road From Damascus

RENATA LIWSKA

Class Photo

Old School is a book featuring art inspired by the aesthetics of 20th century education. I took my inspiration from an old class photo and memories of that time. I tried to retain the expressions and body language of the children, but substituted them with little critters. In the original photo there were children's drawings of soldiers liberating Poland in WWII.

RENATA LIWSKA

Momma Panda

The inspiration for this little panda grew from viewing pandas on the Internet. There I was able to watch the adventures and misadventures of panda cubs up close. I saw their first steps and first taste of bamboo, as well as the first tree they climbed—and the first tree they fell from.

MATT MAHURIN
Anson's Way

BEATRIZ MARTIN-VIDAL
Witch

Witch was conceived to illustrate an ancient Russian tale about a young witch who killed families in the dead of night. My first approach was to adhere closely to the text, which was to depict the young witch, dressed as a Russian peasant, near the house of the people she intended to kill. But, as I developed several sketches, the image was progressively simplified, and, in the final version, I kept just three elements: the woman, the trees, and the skulls. The literal elements became symbolic as I preferred to show the fear—the essence of the tale.

JOHN MATTOS
Pablo's Cantina

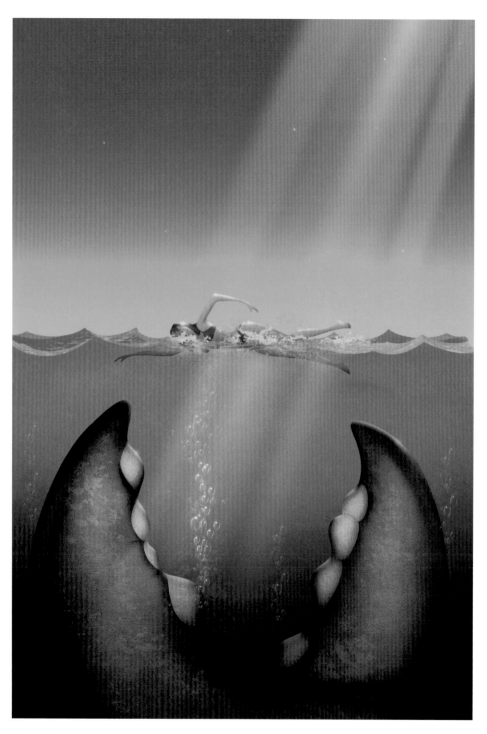

BILL MAYER
Atomic Lobster
This is, of course, a spoof on the famous Jaws poster from the 1975 blockbuster film about a great white shark terrorizing a summer resort community. Mine, however, has the girl in a bathing suit. Oh yeah, and then there's no shark.

WENDELL MINOR
Abraham Lincoln Comes Home

WENDELL MINOR
Pitcher Shower

WENDELL MINOR
Last Polar Bear

WENDELL MINOR
South of Broad

LUC MELANSON
Art Lovers
This is my contribution to the *Work/Life* book, a directory of Canadian illustration and photography. I used an idea from one of my sketchbooks.

LUC MELANSON

My Great Big Mamma 2
This is from a picture book, *My Great Big Mamma*, previously published in French as *Une maman tout entière*. It's a story about a young child who knows that people should be loved for being exactly who and what they are.

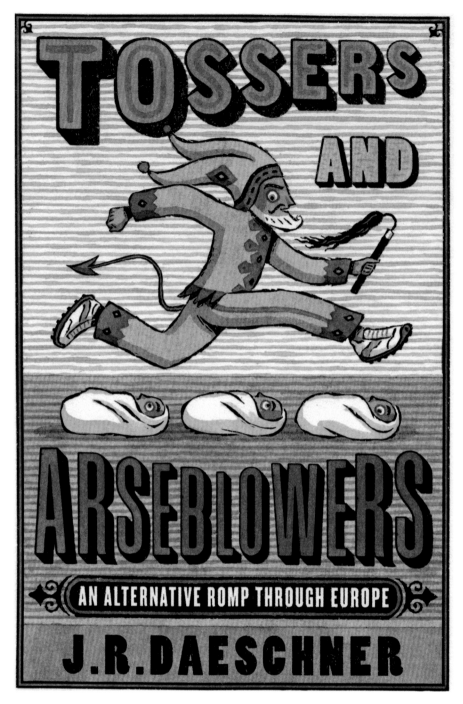

ADAM McCAULEY
Tossers and Arseblowers
This was the cover for a non-fiction travel book, published in the U.K. Its focus was to find unusual events and locales while traveling through Europe. The image on the cover refers to an annual event in Castrillo de Murcia, Spain, called "The Baby-Jumping Colacho Festival." The belief is that when the devil leaps over the newborns, he takes all of the evil along with him. Yes, they do wear devil suits with sneakers!

PEP MONTSERRAT
Greek Myths 2—Orpheus

Orpheus is one of the several stories from old Greek tales retold in *The McElderry Book of Greek Myths* written by Eric Kimmel and published by Simon & Schuster. This version of some of the most ancient stories uses a very modern, contemporary language, so I tried to follow up with a similar visual approach that would be understandable for today's reader.

PEP MONTSERRAT

Odyssey—Calypso, Laertes

This version of *The Odyssey* for young readers was written in Catalan by Albert Jané. He used a very sophisticated language for the story and I had to follow up with the same level of sophistication for the images. My characters are monumental to show the grandiosity of the story. I used mixed media to describe different levels of meaning in Odysseus's story, from simple action to portraying complicated feelings such as questions of life and death—which are not always easy to grasp by young readers.

Yan Nascimbene
Les Deux Anniversaires

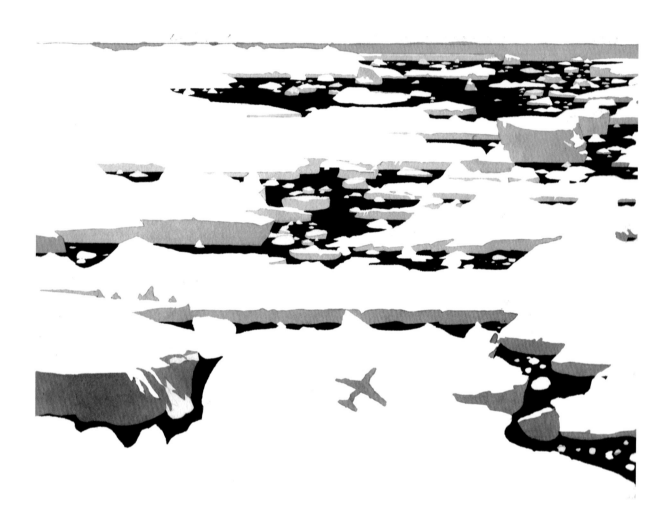

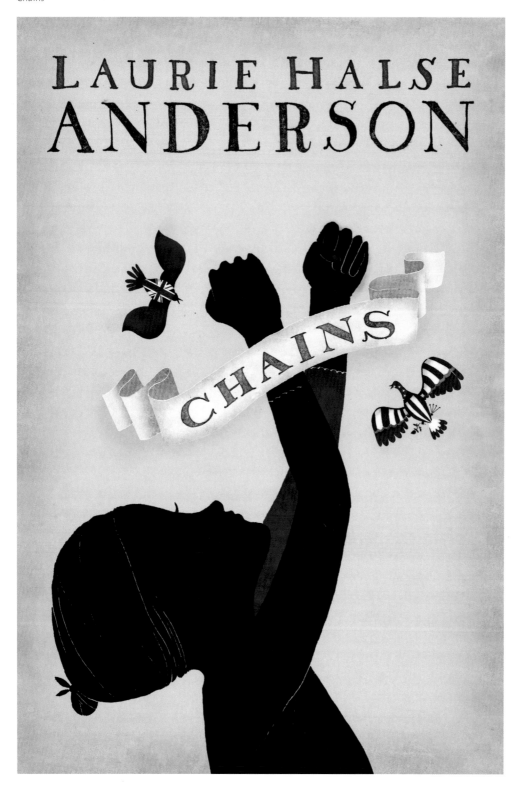

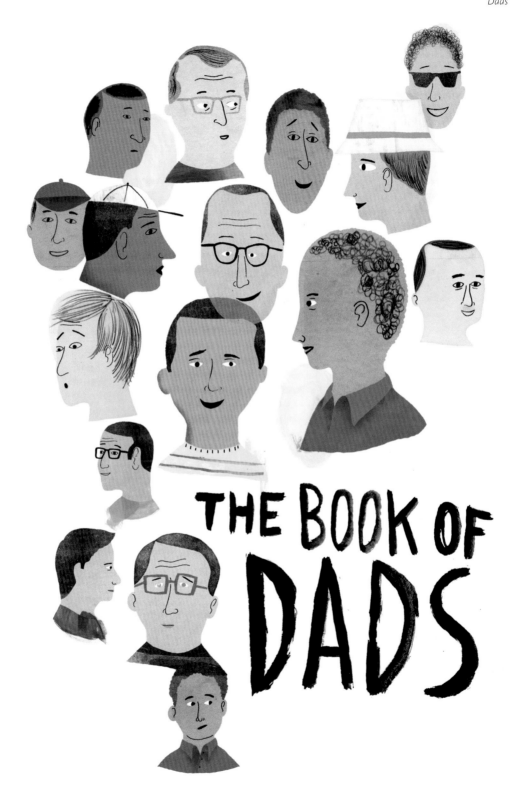

THE BOOK OF DADS

KADIR NELSON

Gus Greenlee

Gus Greenlee was the "numbers king" in Pittsburgh during the Great Depression. He's shown here seated at a booth in his snazzy restaurant, the Crawford Grill, counting his daily take. At the time I painted Gus, I was heavily addicted to the HBO drama, *The Sopranos*. The lead actor, James Gandolfini, who played Tony Soprano, was a big inspiration for this painting. The two share a smugness that seemed appropriate for the piece. Gus has the posture of a lion that has just downed his prey, daring you to try to steal a taste.

KADIR NELSON
Low and Away

I was so excited to work on this painting of Slim Jones pitching at Yankee Stadium that I forgot to flop my reference photo (Slim was a southpaw). I didn't realize my huge mistake until years later. Fortunately, the painting is not labeled in the book. Phew! But embarrassing nonetheless. The painting depicts an historic contest between rivals Slim Jones and Satchel Paige. The two battled to a tie, a game that was eventually called due to darkness.

KADIR NELSON

ABE-floatboat

Most of us who grew up in American have become familiar with heroic images of Abraham Lincoln sitting or standing on a pedestal, or perhaps, frozen on a coin. Through my research, I came to admire Lincoln, faults and all. I found it very interesting that as a young man, despite his very thin and long build, Lincoln was quite physically strong. I wanted to show a bit of this in this painting. Here too, Lincoln strikes a very heroic pose, set against a dramatic sky. I couldn't help myself.

KADIR NELSON
Safe at Home

This painting depicts Jackie Robinson of the Kansas City Monarchs safely stealing home during a Monarch home game in 1945, his only season in the Negro Leagues. The following year Robinson signed with the Brooklyn Dodgers and played a year with the Montreal Royals before integrating Major League Baseball in 1947. This image would have been impossible to photograph because, to increase the drama of the moment, I chose to show everything happening at once— i.e., Jackie sliding, the ball coming in, the batter stepping back, and the ump making the call.

DOUG MOSS

A Christmas Tail 2

This illustration is part of a holiday storybook that our company wrote, illustrated, printed, and distributed to clients as gifts. The staff also sold the book to raise funds for needy families. The mice in the illustration are working together to complete a seemingly impossible project for one of Santa's elves.

TIM O'BRIEN
Mayor

Some of the best assignments I have received over the past few years have been for Jeanne Lee at Simon & Schuster. She repackages classic novels and I have done some great titles. This one is for Thomas Hardy's *The Mayor of Casterbridge*. Its subtitle says it all: *The life and death of a man of character*. I liked the idea of a frozen moment of recognition in a life of mistakes. I originally had thought Brian Rhea might be a good model for this but I look like I've made more mistakes, hence I'm it.

ZACHARIAH O'HORA
Live Poultry Slaughter
This was for a book project by Julia Breckenreid that illustrated places in New York, either real or imagined. This is a real place, right across from my studio in Greenpoint.

Eric Orchard

Guardian of Autumn

This piece was done for the Totoro Forest Project, a fund-raising auction and exhibition to support Totoro Forest Foundation, the trust created by filmmaker Hayao Miyazaki. I chose to portray a forest spirit who resides along the coast of my native Nova Scotia. It was done with graphite and white ink on Arches Hot Press paper.

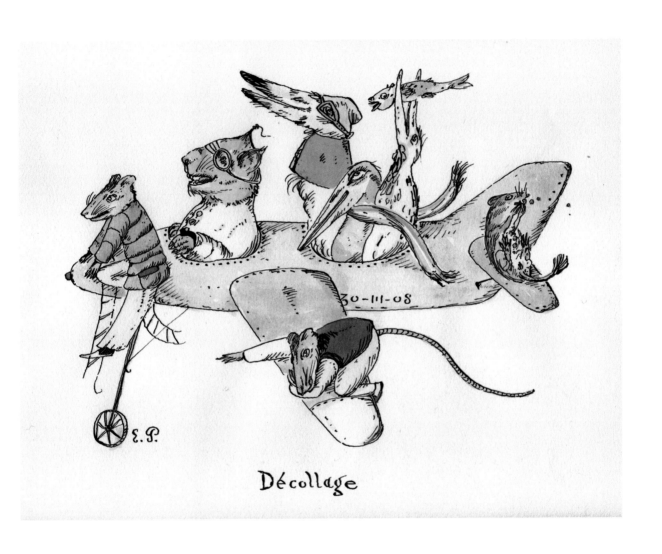

Décollage

EMMANUEL PIERRE
Decollage (Take Off)

CHRIS RAHN
The Chinese Parrot

This is the cover of the second book in the re-release of the Charlie Chan detective series. It's a classic detective mystery about a murder whose only witness is a parrot. I had a great time exploring the styles of that period and trying to lend the cover the sort of Film Noir moodiness so characteristic of the pulp novels of the '20s and '30s.

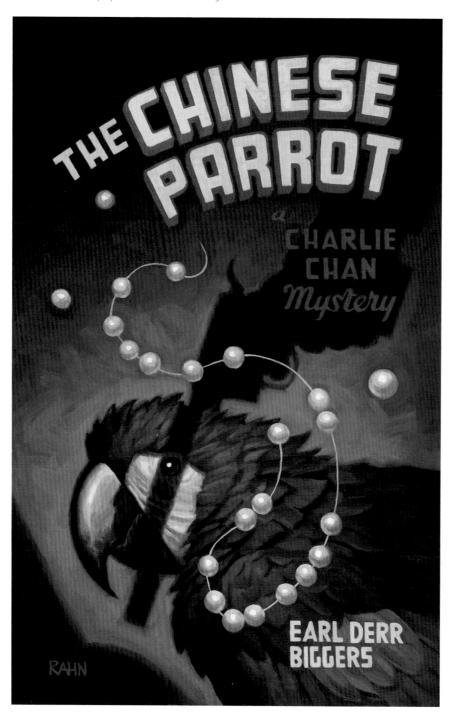

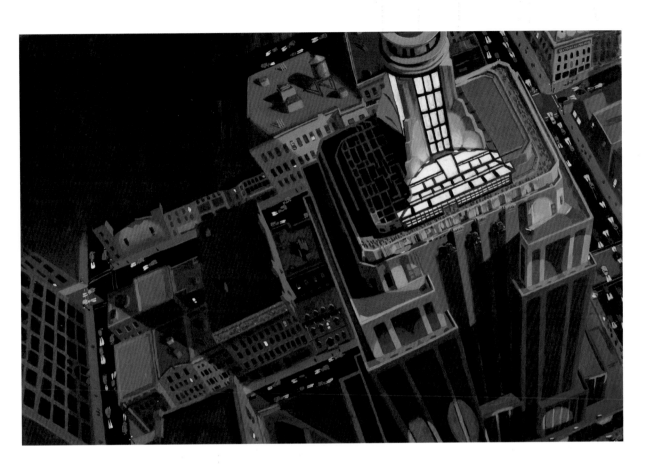

JAMES RANSOME
Empire State Building

This illustration was done for a book entitled *Skyboys*, a story of how the Empire State Building was built. My idea was to show the Empire State Building on the night it was completed and how it loomed over New York City. The most difficult part was envisioning the building at night in 1931, when it wasn't illuminated in the way we are accustomed to seeing today. Those lights were not added until the 1940s. So, I put spotlights on the ground shining up illuminating parts of the building. It was a lot of fun "faking" what these spotlights on the ground would have looked like.

ANDY RASH

Superhero School Reflection

Leonard was very excited to attend *Superhero School* (the new picture book written by Aaron Reynolds and published by Bloomsbury USA), but that was before he realized he would be spending his entire time studying math! How can anyone concentrate on fractions when there is so much real superwork to be done? This illustration shows Leonard and a schoolmate in class with their teacher, The Blue Tornado. It's hard to listen to a lecture when there's a giant marauding robot outside! The image is a digital composite of several Sharpie drawings and textures created with gouache.

ONE OUT, LAST of the NINth...

RalphBranca PITCHES,

Thomson takes a strike

called on the inside corner

Bobby hitting at .292 He's had a single and a double and he drove in the GIANTS first run with a long fly to center... Brooklyn leads it 4 to 2 Runner down the Line at third. Not taking any chances...

Branca throws...

PAUL ROGERS

Ralph Branca

American Express produced a book with portraits and feature articles about some of their charter members. I was asked to do a portrait of Ralph Branca. He's the Brooklyn Dodger pitcher who delivered the pitch to Bobby Thomson that became known as "The Shot Heard 'Round The World" in a playoff for the pennant in 1951. I drew the fatal moment Branca delivered the pitch. The game, played at The Polo Grounds, has taken on legendary status in baseball history, and

fans have been talking about it ever since. Should Branca have walked Thomson with first base open and pitched to the rookie Willie Mays? Did Giant coach Herman Franks steal pitching signs with a telescope from the centerfield clubhouse and relay them to Thomson? Russ Hodges' famous play-by-play call was recorded off the television by a fan at home. And what happened to the ball?

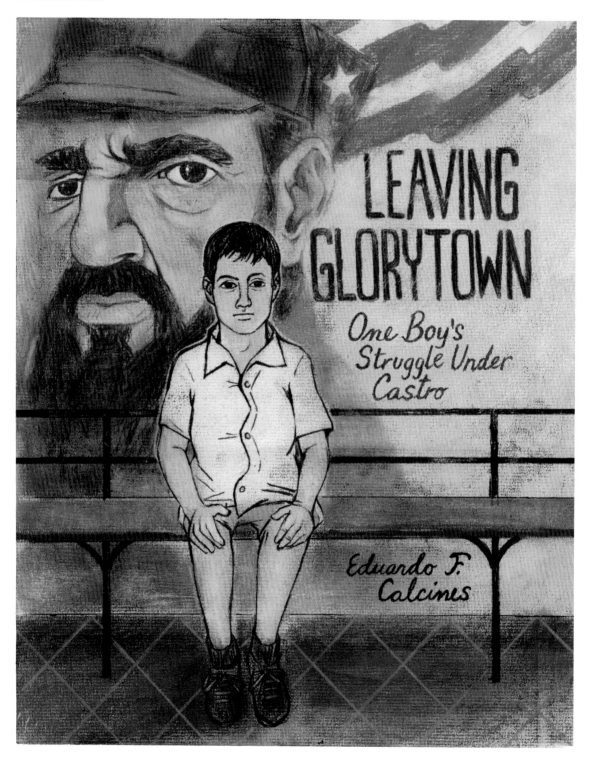

Edel Rodriguez
A Dog in a Hat
Cover for *A Dog in a Hat*, a book about the professional cycling circuit
in Belgium.

RACHEL SALOMON
Elegy for Easterly
This image was created for the book *Elegy for Easterly*, a book of short stories by Zimbabwean author Petina Gappah. The piece was done in acrylic, ink, and graphite.

RUTH SANDERSON

Mother Goose

This painting was created for the first spread in my picture book, *Mother Goose and Friends*. It illustrates the rhyme "Old Mother Goose," which simply says that she rides on a gander, and lives in a house built in a wood. Since I have a background in illustrating fairytales, I wanted to bring that influence to my version of Mother Goose. So I thought I'd add a magical touch and have some elves cleaning the house, which happens to be built onto a tree, and some fairies playing outside, riding goslings, etc. My medium is oil on panel. The painting took about three weeks to paint.

YUKO SHIMIZU
Sandman Cover

STEVE SIMPSON
Mr. Brown

The illustration was created for an AB-CD book, an alphabet book with a CD of songs. Each page was created by an illustrator from a different country. Each illustrator was paired with a writer and musician. The artwork was drawn in pencil and rendered in Photoshop. I chose three strong colors with a retro feel and later added texture and splatter. The client is Stichting Culturele Droomwevers in Amsterdam.

RICHARD TUSCHMAN

Smoke Book Jacket

Smoke, a middle-grade novel by Mavis Jukes, tells the story of a twelve-year-old boy, Colton, and his black Maine Coon cat, Smoke. At one point in the book, Smoke runs away from their home in rural California. For the cover illustration, I imagined Smoke in his travels, sitting on a fencepost, surveying the countryside, and tried to convey a melancholic mood reflecting the story's themes of longing and separation. Many thanks to my cat, Smithers, for posing for the digital montage.

JACK UNRUH
George Bush Playing Ping Pong
Papa George kept a diary of his adventures as an ambassador to China. I know it's a bit difficult to play ping-pong in this outfit, but he insisted, and who am I to argue with a former head of the CIA, Ambassador to China, and President of the U.S. (also father of George W., which mostly negates the previous achievements).

SAM WEBER
House of Mystery 1

SAM WEBER
13 Orphans

ALAN WITSCHONKE

Stonemasons at Work

These two illustrations are from *Taj Mahal*, my newest book for Mikaya Press. It is my fifth book for this client. Mikaya specializes in non-fiction children's literature and each book in this series highlights one of the man-made Wonders of the World. *Taj Mahal* was a difficult project for me because I challenged myself to develop a new style specifically for this book based on the art of the Mughal Empire, which was in power when the monument was built. I loved pushing my design and compositional skills and creating a hybrid of Eastern and Western perspective. The medium I used was watercolor dyes so that I could achieve a high degree of color saturation and brilliance.

MATTHEW WOOD
The Rose and the Beast

This illustration is inspired by a single page of text from Francesca Lia Block's book, *The Rose and the Beast*. Her book retells familiar fairytales, both surreal and obscure, that are filled with delicate, evocative language. Block explores the elements of love and terror that often fill fairytales, yet she puts on display just how primal these stories are. These were the qualities that I attempted to depict in this illustration. I was hoping that egg tempera's mysterious and delicate nature would best communicate the mood of her stories.

EUGENE YELCHIN

Ghost Files: The Ghost of Japan or Hell Hath No Fury Like a Mad Yure!
The concept for *Ghost Files: The Haunting Truth* was that it was written by ghosts. This is revealed slowly, chapter by chapter. I designed the book in such a way that the reader must physically interact with the book. In this way the mysteries of the supernatural world are revealed. In the *Ghost of Japan* chapter, the demons described in the text become fully visible only after the reader lifts and turns two vertical flaps. I utilized the shape of a Japanese screen for the spread, and then painted the demons on the vertical panels in the style of nineteen-century woodblock prints.

UNCOMMISSIONED

SCOTT BAKAL
ILLUSTRATOR

Award-winning illustrator Scott Bakal won a Silver Medal from the Society of Illustrators 50th Annual for an image in his book *Me & the Devil*. The art from this book has received over 20 recognitions and an additional two medals. Scott's work has been accepted by *American Illustration*, *3x3*, *Spectrum*, and *Communication Arts*. His work appears in *The Wall Street Journal*, *The Washington Post*, *The New Republic*, *Yoga Journal*, *Discover Magazine*, and a host of others. He can be found drawing incessantly in his sketchbooks, creating paintings for exhibitions, teaching illustration, and lecturing at art schools around the country. Scott lives and works in New York City.

RICHARD BERENSON
BERENSON DESIGN & BOOKS, LLC

Specializing in book packaging and editorial design, Berenson Design & Books, LLC produces graphics for publishers, packagers, and non-profits. Previously, Richard Berenson worked at the Reader's Digest Association for over 25 years, first as managing art director for the trade book division. Directly responsible for the design of numerous illustrated reference books, he purchased over $1 million worth of illustration. Then, as Worldwide Art Director for *Reader's Digest* magazine, he supervised the design and acquisition of all illustration for the U.S. magazine and 48 international editions. Richard was an instructor at the Art Students League of New York and is a member of the executive committee and board of directors of the Society of Illustrators. He recently served four terms as president and is presently co-chair of the Long-Range Planning and Community Services committees, and also serves on the Permanent Collection committee.

SUE COE
ILLUSTRATOR

One of the foremost political artists working today, Sue Coe was born in England in 1951. She moved to New York in the early '70s and in the following years, her work was featured in numerous museum collections and exhibitions, including a retrospective at the Hirshhorn Museum in Washington. Sue is a firm believer in the power of the media to affect change, and her work has been published in countless periodicals. Similarly, she sees printmaking as a way to reach a broad audience and has spent years documenting the atrocities committed by people against animals. "Elephants We Must Never Forget: New Paintings, Drawings and Prints by Sue Coe," is her latest series. Previous publications include *How to Commit Suicide in South Africa* (1983), *X* (1986), *Police State* (1987), *Dead Meat* (1996), *Pit's Letter* (2000), *Bully! Master of the Global Merry-Go-Round* (2004), and *Sheep of Fools...A Song Cycle for Five Voices* (2005).

PAUL DAVIS
ILLUSTRATOR

Born in Oklahoma in 1938, Paul Davis won a scholarship to the School of Visual Arts in New York at age 17, and later joined Push Pin Studios. He struck out on his own in 1963, his distinctive work influencing many illustrators from then on. Paul served as art director for Joseph Papp's Public Theater, and his iconic poster for *The Threepenny Opera* is in MoMA's collection. His paintings for advertising, publishing, and theater have been the subject of museum exhibitions in the U.S., Europe, and Japan. He has earned many awards, including honorary doctorates from the School of Visual Arts and the Maryland Institute College of Arts; the coveted AIGA Medal; The Art Directors Club Hall of Fame, and, in 2009, the Society of Illustrators Hall of Fame. He is a Fellow of the American Academy in Rome.

STEFANO IMBERT
ILLUSTRATOR

Stefano Imbert was born and raised in Rome, Italy, where he studied at the Istituto d'Arte. In 2002 he graduated from the School of Visual Arts in New York City. Passion for his projects gives his work an emotional range, from pathos to the whimsical, and throughout many of his images, one may detect his ever-present sense of humor. He has provided poster design and illustration for theaters nationwide, including Hartford Stage Company, Mint Theater Company, Boomerang Theatre Company, and BC/EFA. Stefano has provided cover art internationally for Oxford University Press, Simon & Schuster, Broadway Play Publishing, and Light Hunter Publications, among others. A member of the Society of Illustrators since 2003, he has served on its board of directors as International Chair since 2004.

RUTH MARTEN
ILLUSTRATOR

Ruth Marten has had a wideranging artistic career doing illustration, fashion drawing, tattooing, and is now devoting all her energies to fine arts. Best known for her covers for the Peter Mayle Provence books, she works in many styles. A native New Yorker, she has been showing her peculiar and perverse pictures in London, where she will be included in the Charles Saatchi Collection exhibit in 2009.

CHRIS SILAS NEAL
ILLUSTRATOR

Chris Silas Neal was born in Texas and raised in Florida and Colorado. He studied music and advertising at the University of Colorado in Boulder before moving to New York to pursue a career in illustration. His work has been published by a variety of magazines and book publishers, and his recent fiction and non-fiction cover art is featured in the AIGA's permanent collection of design. His clients include advertising agencies such as Chiat/Day and Arnold Worldwide, Sub Pop records, Knopf, HarperCollins, FSG, and *The New York Times*, where he illustrates the "Modern Love" column every Sunday. He works and lives in Brooklyn and teaches illustration at Pratt.

BRUCE WALDMAN
ILLUSTRATOR

For more than 25 years Bruce Waldman has been working as a printmaker and illustrator in New York City, and teaching at the School of Visual Arts. His etchings and monoprints have been exhibited both nationally and internationally, and are in the permanent collections of the Metropolitan Museum of Art; the Library of Congress in Washington, DC; the Royal Collection in London; and the Franklin Mint Collection in Pennsylvania; as well as in many other private and corporate collections. Bruce illustrated the cover for the 1990 national bestseller *Iron John* by Robert Bly, and won the Silver Medal in the book category of the Society of Illustrators 45th Annual. He has illustrated more then 20 books, including seven for the Franklin Library. Bruce is a member of the board of governors of the Printmaking Workshop, and a director of The New York Society of Etchers.

Song

This piece, entitled *Song*, stemmed from a series of artworks that expressed the interconnection between music and the human body—a subject very familiar to me as I have been a musician nearly all my life. I eventually began to explore the experience of music from the perspective of one who could not hear. Some musicians can hear music in their minds so well that there may be little to no difference between the actual sound of music and what they experience in their head. This is how musicians who have lost their hearing can still write and perform music, since it is experienced firstly, and accurately, in their minds.

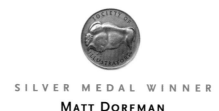

Loudmouth
This is part of a personal series I began at home in order to combine divergent stylistic tendencies that I'd been demonstrating in my sketchbooks. A good bit of my uncommissioned work concerns the subconscious motives behind common social behaviors. Since this piece was created with a second painting in mind, one that concerned an unseemly know-it-all, *Loudmouth* was a self-made opportunity to harangue that special personality you sometimes meet who's great at talking loudly, but can't listen for squat. I suppose the piece comes from a place of bitterness, but ultimately, I'd rather paint than start a bar fight.

Please Wash Your Hands
This started out as a small drawing in my sketchbook when I was going through a period of drawing a lot of microorganisms. And now we come in contact with microorganisms on a daily basis—not that I'm a serial hand washer or anything. Now, if I can just find a way to get prints of this painting into a small percentage of the washrooms of restaurants in this country, my wife and I would be able to retire—along with great gobs of SPF 50 sunscreen—to the Caribbean.

SILVER MEDAL WINNER
Jack Unruh

Self Portrait
You know all those reference shots I take of my hands, arms, and other body parts? Well there's always a detached head in the background—extra stuff never used. So I picked one and had some fun. Being a bit vain, I tried to make me look better than I really am.

A. RICHARD ALLEN
The Wire
This image was a self-promotional portrait piece depicting a scene
between two characters from the HBO TV drama, *The Wire*.

Scott Bakal
William Shakespeare

ANA BENAROYA
Crazy Head
This piece was actually the result of using scraps and leftover paint. I have the habit of using scrap paper or canvas paper as palettes for my acrylic paints, and one day I decided to try turning some of them into pieces themselves. I kept the background colors as they were and simply added facial features to create a series of these crazy heads.

BARRY BRUNER

Dictators!

The Dictators! project was a personal exploration into the extremes of the dark side of human nature. It started simply as a self-promotion piece that would feature the portraits of many past and current leaders that fall into the infamous dictator category. But as people caught wind of what I was doing, it began to turn into a huge collaborative project.

Currently I'm working with a few writers to put these drawings into a book. The Mugabe drawing has since been used to make satirical propaganda posters. I can't wait to see where this project ends up and to see what other future projects it might spawn.

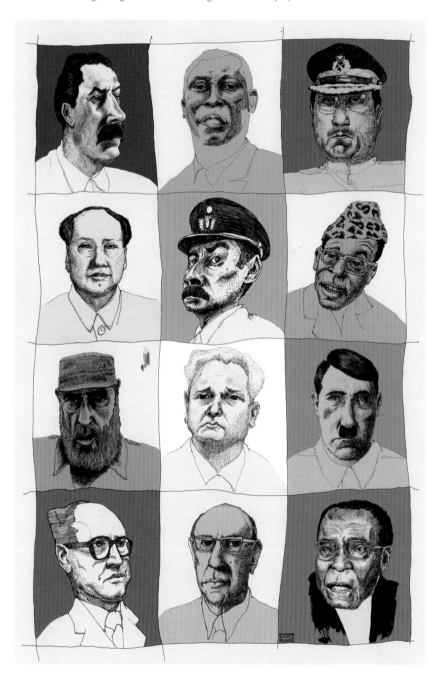

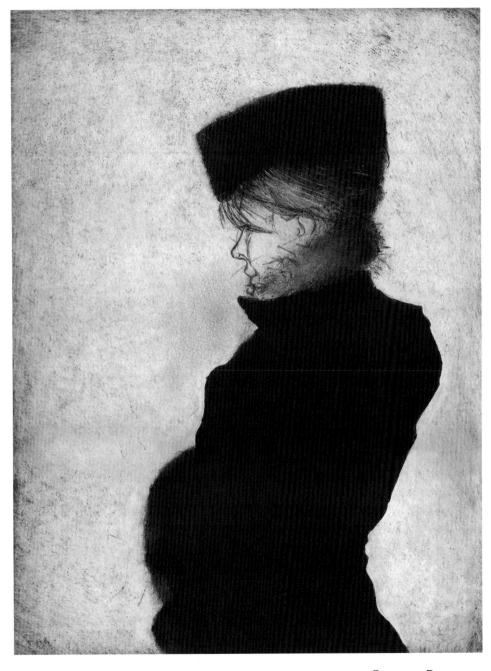

RACHEL BURGESS
She Cuts A Gallant Show

MARC BURCKHARDT
Mirror
Titled *Mirror*, this is one of a series of allegorical paintings done for the
Marder Gallery in Bridgehampton.

MARC BURCKHARDT
Green
This piece was for an exhibition curated by Mark Murphy, loosely arranged around the theme of "Green." I was inspired by an island of trees I sketched one afternoon in Englischer Park, in Munich.

MARK BURRIER

Handmaze Print

While driving home one evening I thought of an image of a hand made completely of maze-like, interwoven lines. Once home, I sat down with a piece of paper, a pen, and a cup of tea and started the maze. Line after line the piece came together in one take. I enlarged and silkscreened the image in two colors onto Starch Mint French Paper. The print is sold on my website.

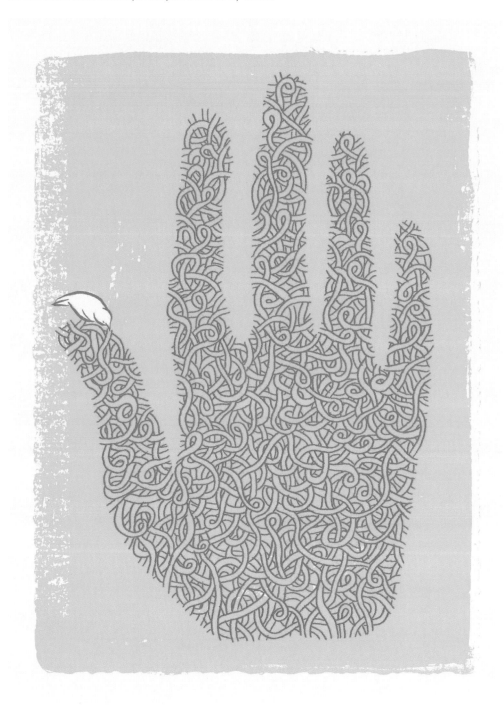

Q. Cassetti

Memento Mori Study

Memento mori is a Latin phrase meaning "Be mindful of death," which may be translated as "Remember that you are mortal," "Remember you will die," "Remember that you must die," or "Remember your death." I turned 50 and mortality changed focus for me. I used a daily exploration of death and transition through ink drawings and reading—remembering my mortality in a deliberate way. My inspiration came from the death and mourning customs, traditions, grave markers, and stone carvings of the early New England Puritan colonists and those of the Victorians. This willow skull blends the skull, an obvious symbol of death, with that of the willow tree, which represents regeneration and growth because of its ability to constantly regenerate. With death, there is life.

JOHN CUNEO

Watching

This is a small sketchbook thing. I was thinking about reading, while drawing in a pad on my lap and listening to the television. At the risk of getting too technical, I should explain that the rendering of the large face in the doorway was achieved by carefully rotating the entire sketch pad approximately 90 degrees.

PAUL DAVIS
Lucille

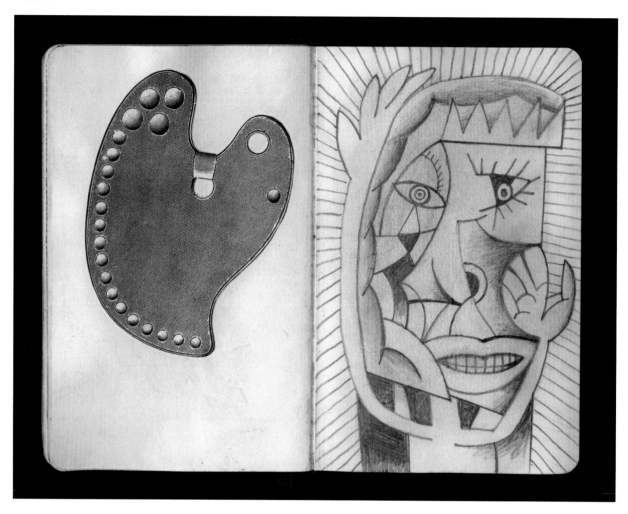

MICHAEL GLENWOOD
Give Peace a Chance

RICHARD A. GOLDBERG

Lion Drawing
The general line is, that the lion shall lie down with the sheep. The lion's
line here IS the sheep.

RICH GUZMAN
Casual Friday Penguin

This piece is part of a series for a printmaking thesis, that focuses on the idea of various animals taking advantage of a "casual day" and opting to dress as any other mammal. I tried to pick as diverse a pair of animals as possible to create something unique and previously unseen, choosing the remote penguin and the mainland deer. The black layer was drawn first on acetate with Rapidograph and the colors were then cut separately on Rubylith film. The colors conform to a scheme that was used throughout the rest of the series.

TATSURO KIUCHI

The Apple Store in Ginza
This was my personal piece for a group exhibition titled *Ginza*, organized by the Tokyo Illustrators Society. All members of the society were asked to do a piece dealing with anything about Ginza (the well-known city in Tokyo). I depicted the Apple store there. The piece is digitally created with Photoshop.

JORGE MASCARENHAS
The Bachelor
Generally, when I work I like to have noise around, whether from the TV or radio. This idea came to me from the popular TV show, *The Bachelor*. Although the man in this picture is not a self-portrait, the women are based on reality. Loved or hated, these women had their unique, memorable traits. All portraits were 11" x 16", painted on illustration board, and put together digitally.

LUC MELANSON

Picasso

I've been doing portraits in my sketchbooks for a year or so—something I have
never done before. This is the first one to become a finished illustration.

Luc Melanson

Clear Cuts
Another idea from my sketchbook. It took me about ten minutes to do the final version.

HAL MAYFORTH

Reading Makes You Less Stupid

ROBERT RENDO
Denial is Just a Six Letter Word

In this piece, I drew inspiration from Gregory Smith, former director of the Royalty-in-Kind Program, a division of a federal agency that holds oil reserves and sells them on the open market to energy companies. In 2008, whistle blowers launched an investigation into Mr. Smith's department, outing Mr. Smith's regular use of marijuana with oil executives and his systematic cocaine purchases from his secretary.

Mr. Smith's lawyer, Steven Peters, maintained that despite Mr. Smith's cocaine habit, he was nonetheless "a dedicated employee for more than 28 years" and "is very proud of what he accomplished." Equally strange was a Justice Department spokeswoman's unwillingness to explain why federal prosecutors would not be charging Mr. Smith, citing it as an open and shut matter of departmental policy.

Ai Tatebayashi
Chandelier Girl

Because it was my thesis project at the School of Visual Arts, I have been illustrating women's issues since my college years. Normally, I come up with ideas by getting inspired by books, films, fashions, and, of course, my own life experience as a woman. This illustration, *Chan-* *delier Girl*, is not for a particular story or idea. I think this image is showing various aspects of women's issues comprehensively. Each viewer can interpret the concepts or story differently by looking at Chandelier Girl's situations, the look, the feeling, etc.

Michael Wandelmaier
Harpooning the Wooly Whale
This illustration sprung to mind while researching mythical monsters for
another project. I liked the idea of casting the archetypal sea-monster as a
tragic character in a story where man is the aggressor. There's something
sinister about the Robinson Crusoe-esque sailors banding together to
hunt this furry leviathan, yet it's unclear from the image who will come
out of this confrontation the winner.

SEQUENTIAL

SEQUENTIAL JURY

MEGAN MONTAGUE CASH
ILLUSTRATOR

Megan Montague Cash is an illustrator, designer, and author who specializes in work for children. Her clients have ranged from the Museum of Modern Art to Nickelodeon, and projects have included award-winning toys, games, paper engineered products, corporate identities, and exhibit designs. She has published numerous children's books, including *What Makes the Seasons?* (Viking), which was turned into an exhibit at the Discovery Gateway museum. As well as other honors, Megan collaborated with Mark Newgarden on the picture book *Bow-Wow Bugs a Bug* (Harcourt), which won a Gold Medal in the Society of Illustrators' Original Art Show in 2007. She teaches at Pratt Institute and lives in Brooklyn with a cartoonist, a dog, and two cats.

JOAN HILTY
DC COMICS

Joan Hilty is a senior editor at the Vertigo imprint of DC Comics, specializing in graphic novels. She is also a cartoonist whose work has appeared in *The Village Voice*, *Ms.*, and *The ADVOCATE*, and is creator of the syndicated comic strip *Bitter Girl*. She studied art at Brown University and the Rhode Island School of Design, back in the dark days before Photoshop.

BEN KATCHOR
CARTOONIST, AUTHOR

Ben Katchor's books include *The Jew of New York* and *Julius Knipl, Real-Estate Photographer*. He produces a monthly strip for *Metropolis* magazine. *The Slug Bearers of Kayrol Island*, his most recent music-theater collaboration with composer Mark Mulcahy, won an Obie Award. He lives in New York City and is on the faculty of Parsons The New School.

MARK NEWGARDEN
CARTOONIST

Among his various and sundry careers, cartoonist Mark Newgarden has worked as a concoctor of novelties (Garbage Pail Kids), a graphic artist (from *Raw* magazine to *The New York Times*), and a writer for TV, film, and multimedia projects (from Microsoft to Cartoon Network). His work has also graced such venues as the Smithsonian Institute, the Cooper-Hewitt, the Brooklyn Museum, The Art Institute of Chicago, and the Institute of Contemporary Arts in London. He is the author of *Cheap Laffs*, a picture history of novelty items published by Abrams, and *We All Die Alone*, a collection of his comics and humor from Fantagraphics Books. His first children's book, *Bow-Wow Bugs a Bug* (with Megan Montague Cash) was released in June 2007 by Harcourt and won a Gold Medal from the Society of Illustrators.

LEIF PARSONS
ILLUSTRATOR

Leif Parsons was educated in Canada and New York and has degrees in philosophy and design. He has been working as an illustrator for a number of years and has been published by a variety of editorial and commercial clients. He simultaneously has been executing personal work, which has been shown on both coasts. Leif has recently been focused on trying to find the fine line between looseness and tightness, between deliberate idea and spontaneous expression, between observation and imagination. He is also curious as to how many times he can draw himself naked and get it published in *The New York Times* (three so far).

JEFF SCHER
FEZ FILMS

Jeff Scher is a painter who makes experimental films and an experimental filmmaker who paints. His work is in the permanent collection of the Museum of Modern Art and the Hirshhorn Museum, and has been screened at the Guggenheim Museum, the Pompidou Center in Paris, the San Francisco Museum of Modern Art, and at many film festivals, including opening night at the New York Film Festival. Jeff has also had two solo shows of his paintings that have also been included in many group shows in New York galleries. Additionally, he has created commissioned work for HBO, HBO Family, PBS, the Sundance Channel and others. He teaches graduate courses at the School of Visual Arts and at NYU Tisch School of the Arts, and also writes a blog for *The New York Times* called *The Animated Life*.

NEIL SWAAB
ILLUSTRATOR, ART DIRECTOR

Neil Swaab is a freelance art director, illustrator, and cartoonist based in Brooklyn. His work has been recognized by the Society of Illustrators, *Communication Arts*, *Print*, and *American Illustration*. His weekly comic strip, *Rehabilitating Mr. Wiggles*, has been collected into two books in America, one book in Italy, and another in Russia. Neil's work can also be seen in the show, *Superjail!* on Adult Swim, in which he served as a character layout artist, creating and drawing many characters for the first season. In addition, he also teaches at Parsons The News School For Design in the illustration program.

SARA VARON
ILLUSTRATOR

Sara Varon is an illustrator, comics artist, and printmaker, currently living in Brooklyn. Her children's books include *Chicken and Cat* (Scholastic Press, 2006) and *Chicken and Cat Clean Up* (Scholastic Press, 2009). Her graphic novels include *Robot Dreams* (First Second Books, 2007), which was named one of the year's 150 best books by *Publisher's Weekly* and one of the year's 40 best children's books by *Kirkus Reviews*. Her illustrations have appeared in *Nickelodeon Magazine*, *The New York Times*, and *The Wall Street Journal*. In addition, Sara teaches silkscreen printing in the Continuing Education department at the School of Visual Arts.

Ergonomics
My assignment was part of an Italian calendar whose general theme was safety. The art director asked if I would do "Ergonomics" and consider doing it as a comic strip. Because I didn't want to deal with translation, I kept it virtually wordless. Sometimes ergonomics can seem like a prissy grade school teacher (Sit up straight! Keep your feet on the floor! Don't mumble!), so I made the instructor rather unsympathetic and strict. I also tend to think of ergonomics in terms of diagrams (the correct viewing angle, wrist angle etc.), so I made the diagrams take over—the comic strip format letting them progressively entangle the "victim." I did the drawing in ink, scanned it into Photoshop, and added color and texture—as well as a ghost image of a plumbing diagram in the background.

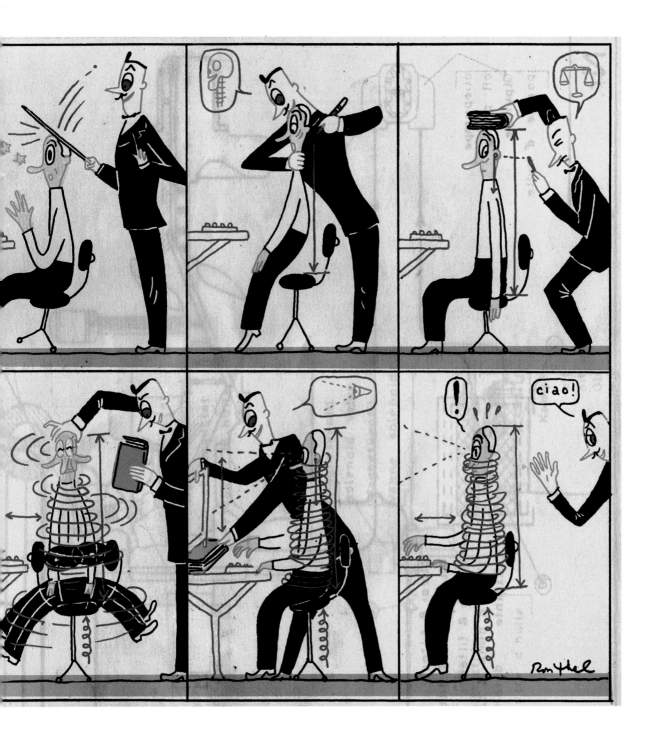

Insurance Myths

In the day-to-day work of being an illustrator, one of the challenges is the act of turning the mundane into something magical. Laura Butler, from *USAA Magazine*, called me with an article about popular insurance myths, including standards like "Are red cars more expensive to insure?" The article itself was built with a dozen smaller paragraphs that addressed different misconceptions about insurance. This led to an idea of illustrating multiple myths, rather than creating a single metaphorical image. Looking for a unique solution of how to put panels in sequence, I stumbled upon an old collection of informational woodcuts about coal mining from the 19th century. They were structured on an unusual grid and were designed as a collective sequence, not a linear narrative. Even though each insurance myth was about very different subject matter, it was easy to find one bit of common ground—the looming portent of disaster. Voila!

SILVER MEDAL WINNER
PETER KUPER

Ceci N'est Pas Une Comic
This is not an artist's statement.

I've learned a lot about the use of images and language over the last eight years and I humbly request you listen to my insight (please ignore the hood and the ropes that bind you to your chair). Fair and balanced news from the no spin zone has informed me that it is better to obey like man's best friend than question questionable actions. Who are we to say what's right and wrong if might makes right and evildoers are hiding behind every water bottle? Since every dog has his day, then surely the inheriting meek will fix everything on earth. So Madoff made off with 50 billion, so what? After a 700 billion dollar bailout, our Titanic nation is shipshape and ready to take on the icebergs (thanks to global warming, they're much smaller). Please don't misunderestimate me—I, for one, am optimistic. After all, the world always needs comics.

MONIKA AICHELE

Everybody Always Thinks They Are Right

Stefan Sagmeister asked me to create six big monkey inflatables for the Six Cities Festival in Scotland. He wanted the monkeys to be in black and white and look angry. I loved the challenge of working in 3D liked the fact that they were bigger than the editorial illustrations I usually work on. It allowed for many different perspectives by having the monkeys looking down on me and moving with the wind]—they became real creatures! Meanwhile, they have been shown not only in Scotland but also at Miami Art Basel and at the Deitch Project in New York.

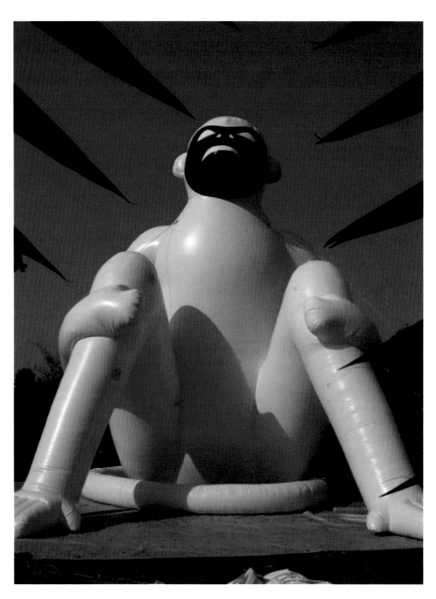

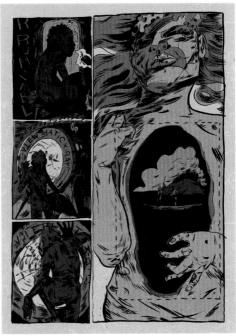

WESLEY ALLSBROOK

The Leviathan

I've always wanted to write a story about a world within a world, each nesting piece related and codependent. The *Leviathan*'s protagonist, a member of a kind of biological clean-up crew, unwittingly finds entry into a second reality by way of an island with a blow-hole. While he wends his way through the paradoxical time/space of this cubist para-

dise, his team struggles to understand, and subsequently destroy, the island which he has come to call home. While the explosion takes the other world back to the deep, along with our protagonist, the island has left something of itself behind.

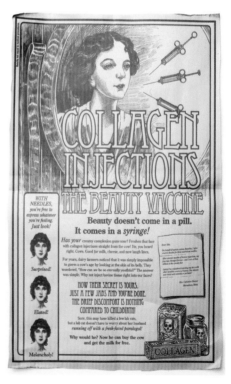

KAKO BERGAMINI
Marianne
Short story based on composer/singer Tori Amos's song *Marianne* for Image Comics' anthology *Comic Book Tattoo*. After knowing the specs of the book (spread page: 11.75" by 23.5") I decided to make a story with few panels and big illustrations. The total area would enhance the

power of the narrative, which would change the pace of the reading, slowing down the turning of pages—like a slow motion sequence in a movie. The idea was to make the reader rest a bit from all the reading and just tag along with the bee.

RAYMOND BIESINGER

Global 500 Industries
For an essay on the ephemeral nature of Los Angeles's physical and metaphysical history.

A POLITICAL Junkie re-emerges on Election DAY to DISCOVER that NOW NOTHING is the SAME...

by STEVE BRODNER

EVERYTHING seemed influenced BY the CAMPAIGN and BEGAN to resemble the candidates. SUDDENLY, #1 TIMES Square seemed to be...OBAMA. and THE ARMY recruiter next DOOR...McCAIN.

Pedicabs...McCAIN

Strollers... OBAMA

JONATHAN BURTON

Project Potato

In collaboration with photographer Sophie Pawlak, this was an experiment in juxtaposing unusual items and imagery, which, in this case, were the content of my fridge and a history of art book. Prints of the work were exhibited in a fine foods boutique in Marseille and were also printed onto decorative ceramic tiles.

Docteur William Fenouil

JONATHAN BURTON

Cover Her Face

The P.D. James novel is a murder mystery set in 1950s England. The commission was for the cover design and seven interior illustrations. The extracts that I chose to illustrate were to reveal some of the clues and red herrings that appear within the detective's investigation. The color used was an emotional response rather than a realistic one and the orange hair color of the murder victim was a constant focus throughout. The only scene where she does not appear, the final "whodunit" image, still has the orange lingering like a ghost. The high viewpoints are there to draw the reader in and give a sense of unease.

BILL CARMAN

Fuzzy Bear Things

Fuzzy Bear Things is a story about fuzzy bear things. It's a story about discovery, life, love (well, actually no love is involved), but plenty of discovery and life. They are done with graphite and acrylic paint on mat board.

JOAN CHIVERTON

Harbor VA Hospital

I'm interested in telling stories visually. So three years ago, I volunteered at the Harbor VA Hospital in Manhattan. For better or worse, it's a place full of stories. I sketched patients and gave them the sketches. In time I started teaching art on a volunteer basis (all art programs were cut six years ago). I began developing stories about various aspects of the hospital. Patients appreciate the visits. And I've gotten other artists involved with patients from Iraq and Afghanistan at Walter Reed Army Medical Center in Washington, DC, as well as older vets at Harbor. The experience has been very rewarding.

Network 3 Prosthetics
PROSTHETIC & SENSORY AIDS
Harbor VA Hospital, New York City

The Pin Men outside
the VA hospital on 23 St.

VETERAN'S CANTEEN
BARBER SERVICE
MONDAY - FRIDAY
8:30 TO 4:00

1090s
SALA
BARBER

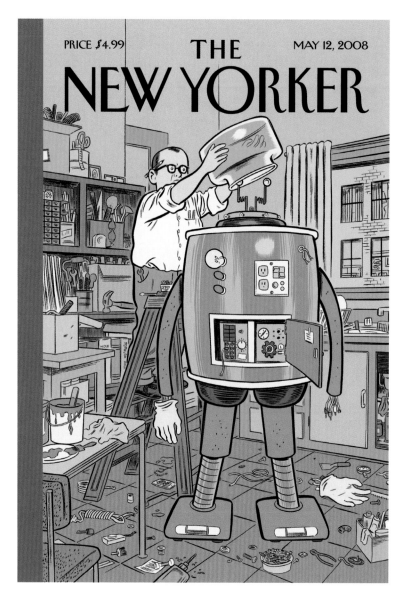

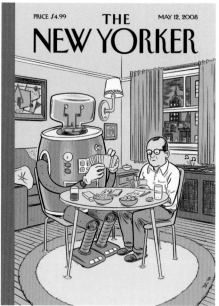

DAN CLOWES
Man's Best Friend

JACQUES DE LOUSTAL
On the Move

LEO ESPINOSA

Otis and Rae and the Grumbling Splunk
A graphic novel-style picture book for children age three to seven written
by Laura Espinosa.

This is Brighton Beach. It is also called Little Russia. Russians love the sea and when they started immigrating to New York in the 70's and 80's, they settled here. Back then, Brighton was desolate and dangerous. Now you can't buy a studio here for less than $400,000.

My mother and I moved to New York from Russia in the early 90's. I hated Brighton when I first saw it. I had come straight from drama school in St.Petersburg, immersed in the worlds of Chekhov and Dostoevsky, and flashy women in fur coats grabbing for kelbasa were the last people I wanted to be associated with. The scene supported many Americans' warped view of Russians.

Pensioners quarreling over their social benefits, youngsters trying too hard to look and feel American, madams stuffed into Gucci, thugs softened up by the surplus of food- all looked vaguely familiar, like a reflection in a crooked mirror. Even the majestic Russian language had mutated here into a concoction of Russian and American slang.

My attitude toward Brighton Beach changed after Karina was born. Even though my American husband doesn't speak a word of Russian, my daughter is fluent. Karina loves coming here. Brighton is a Russian theme park for her. My mother, who says the mix of sea air and restaurant smells is a balm to her soul, loves it too. Now I see the place through the eyes of a five year old and her nostalgic grandmother.

We come here to visit the aquarium, to buy Russian toys and videos,to go to acts at the Millennium Concert Hall. Most important, we come here to buy and eat Russian food.

For the best smoked fish, we go to the "International Food Emporium". Squeezed between display cases filled with delicacies, frantic customers stock up on food as if they were preparing for a great famine. To keep things in order salesladies direct customers: " Woman make your choice. What are you staring at? We are not in the Hermitage." " Lady don't cut in line. Who do you think you are, Catherine the Great?"

On sunny days we go to the boardwalk. Now when I look at the old people, covering the benches like turtles basking under the sun, I can't stop thinking about my grandmother, whom we brought to America at the end of her life. We all lived in the Bronx and she used to take a long subway ride here once a week just to mingle with other old Russians.

Before going home, we stop at Cafe Kashkar-our favorite restaurant. As we reminisce about my childhood in Russia, familiar dishes pile up in front of us: Blood red borshcht, platters of tender lamb and veal kebabs, plates with lightly pickled carrots and eggplant and other delicacies. As I inhale the nostalgic aromas, I can't stop thinking: " I love Brighton Beach."

Yvetta Fedorova

Karina Stories

Karina Stories is a comic strip series started when my client, the Italian magazine, *Internazionale*, asked me to create a comic strip about New York. My daughter Karina was four years old and I was spending a lot of time taking care of her. I decided to create a serious of strips about motherhood in New York. For all my stories I use real locations so people can recognize cafes, playgrounds, and other places they visit with their kids in the city. I like to design the panels in a way that a lot of visuals are cropped and people have to finish the picture in their heads. *Karina Stories* are true stories that come from my daily life with Karina in New York.

ALESSANDRO GOTTARDO

Presidential 2008

The rise of and the campaign for the 2008 presidential race. Hillary versus Obama. Republicans without a good candidate. Four states, four preferences.

Jessie Hartland
Night Shift

Three spreads here from my latest author-illustrated children's picture book, *Night Shift*, about people who work at night. The publisher is Bloomsbury; the medium is gouache. The idea for this book came to me years ago when I was designing store window displays for Barneys and Bloomingdale's.

Brad Holland
Stealing Weather

RYAN INZANA

Brooklyn-ification

This piece is on the subject of gentrification. My happy little crime-plagued neighborhood in Brooklyn had changed, but not necessarily for the better. Old *Twilight Zone* episodes came to mind. The monsters had left Maple Street and were now setting up posh bistros on my block. Neighbors I had known for years disappeared overnight. As is evident in my comic, I haven't any words to suitably explain this phenomenon.

AYA KAKEDA
Delicious Soup of Horror

MICHAEL KLEIN
Alliterative Alphabet Coasters

These images were created for a set of 26 Alliterative Alphabet coasters produced by The Blank Page, a graphic design firm in New York City. Each coaster presented a familiar alliterative phrase comprised of two words. The illustrations were designed to add an element of surprise by providing a somewhat unexpected yet complementary interpretation of each phrase. The images shown were created to accompany the following phrases: Egg Eater, High Hopes, Match Maker, and Short Sheeted.

PETER KUPER

Studs Turkel's Working

This graphic novel is based on Turkel's interviews with workers from all walks of life. For my contribution to this anthology, I chose labor organizer Bill Talcott. Using his words as an anchor, I was free to do more experimental storytelling in the 13-page adaptation. Executed in pen and ink on scratchboard, I felt this was a good medium to evoke labor poster art from the '30s and '40s, which seemed appropriate for the subject.

Andres Vera Martinez
Long, Long, Long

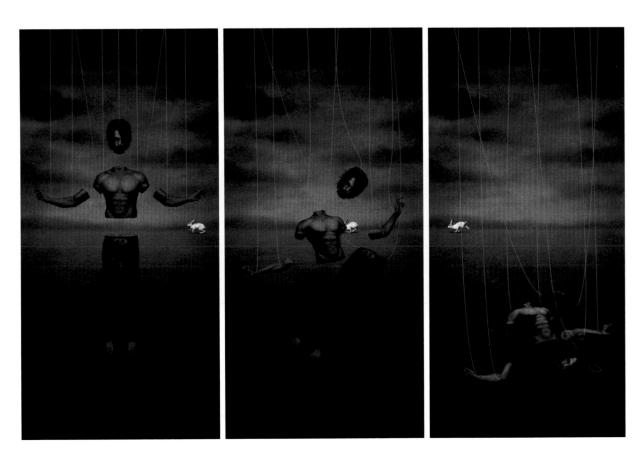

RENÉ MILOT
Lenticular Puppeteer Criss Angel
Lenticular panels for Criss Angel (illusionist of the TV show *Mindfreak*) and Cirque du Soleil, joint venture in Las Vegas at the Luxor Hotel entitled *Believe*. Lenticular technology allows 2D images to move as the viewer moves. The art director wanted to create a room—a hall of paintings to create a sense of things to come for the customers as they proceeded toward the stage. A room full of five, eight-foot-tall framed paintings would move as the person walks by, thereby creating an eerie and surprising displacement of one's comfort level. Working with a great creative team, the main concern was creating such large digital format images within a ridiculous deadline while maintaining a flow of natural movement for each of the lenticular panels.

LEE MOYER

Literary Pin-Ups

The idea for a Literary Pin-Up Calendar came with the very strong reaction to a poster I'd done (digitally) for *Moby Dick—The Musical*. I studied the classics (Elvgren, Petty, Ballantyne), then successfully sought volunteer models from our community in Portland, Oregon. My goal was to produce a series whose women were multi-cultural, competent and, of course, alluring. While these first two may seem obvious, neither has been a Pin-Up staple. Occasionally, Elvgren would let the real features of a South American model seep into his final work, but the number of pin-ups whose dresses have been caught in revolving doors, on fishing lines, by alligators, et al., is legion.

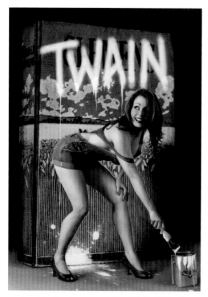

Di Peter Nguyen
The Missive

JAKE PARKER
The Antler Boy

BILL PLYMPTON
Mexican Standoff

JOHN RABOU
Vlaardingen 1018

Four illustrations for *Graven in Vlaardingen*, an archeological exhibition and accompanying publication. Applied as defining elements and putting the artifacts in a historical perspective. One of the first counts of Holland, Dirk III—struggling for independence in the battle of Vlaardingen in 1018—defeated the almighty Germans, who were not familiar with the swampy Dutch river delta. Almost all soldiers were killed or drowned, while they withdrew in panic. Ultimately, this event led to the rise of the powerful County of Holland. Done in watercolor in the style of the very informative, beautiful source created in 1066: the Bayeux Tapestry.

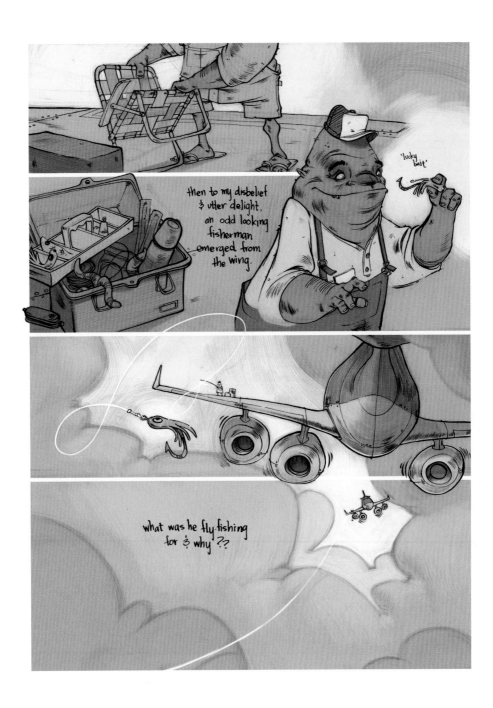

GUILLERMO REAL

Plane Food (Un Cuento)

Plane Food started out as a daydream I had while observing the wing of a plane and asking myself, What if that little latch opened up and a curious looking creature emerged from it? Who would he be? And why would he be there?" I fell in love with trying to answer these questions and visually convey my thoughts.

RED NOSE STUDIO

Environmental Issues

Focusing on how Japan is leading the G-8 in environmental issues, I was able to tie in my fascination with smokestacks and lumberjacks to come up with visuals that communicated the tough job of regulating emissions. The art director was May Wong.

RED NOSE STUDIO

Built To...

This series was created for a Norwegian appliance manufacture whose high-end dishwashers are built to handle the worst of the worst. Usually the characters in my work are the centerpieces and focal points, but in this case the mess on the table needed to steal the show, which gave me a chance to put my prop-making skills to the test. The art directors were Hans Martin Rønneseth and André Koot.

PAOLO RIVERA
Mythos: Captain America

Written by Paul Jenkins, *Mythos: Captain America* recounts the origin story of one of Marvel Comics's first superheroes. The fully painted, 22-page comic book was published in 2008 and recently included in the Mythos Hardcover, a collection of six origin stories starring Marvel's most popular characters. The four pages featured here span the life of Captain America's alter ego, Steve Rogers, from growing up on the Lower East Side to fighting in World War II.

GRAHAM ROUMIEU

Bigfoot: I Not Dead

The third in my series of *Bigfoot* autobiographies. In *I Not Dead*, we find him as arrogant, confused, and short-tempered as ever, but seasoned with a growing realization of mortality.

JIM RUGG
Afrodisiac

Jason Sadler
Sub Plotter

These pages are an excerpt from the short, illustrated story *Sub Plotter* that is part of the *Out of Picture 2* collection. It was designed on paper, cleaned up in Flash and finished in Photoshop. The story takes place during World War II. A young naval officer serving as a map plotter at the British Admiralty accidentally sneezes on a map and thwarts a submarine captain's attempt to sink a British ship. The flat graphic shapes and limited, desaturated color palettes of wartime posters were a strong influence on the final treatment for this piece.

ZINA SAUNDERS

The Party's Over

"The Party's Over" is a series of more than 20 paintings chronicling the 2008 presidential race, spurred by my dismay at the dearth of female illustrators represented in political art and the increasingly bizarre McCain campaign. The paintings are mixed media and were sketched and painted in the very early morning hours before I got to work on my regularly scheduled assignments. The events from the preceding day unfailingly provided abundant material to lampoon.

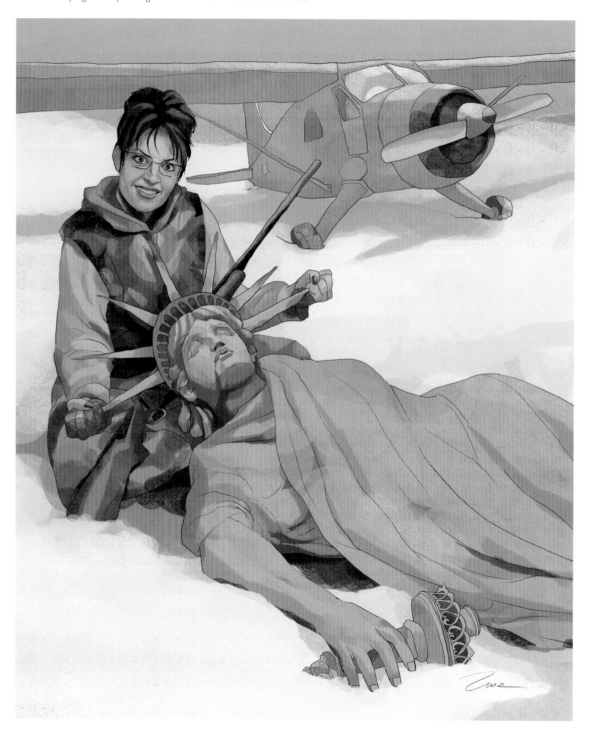

YUKO SHIMIZU
Tiger Beer Billboards

MICHAEL SLOAN

The Travels of Professor Nimbus

The Travels of Professor Nimbus is an ongoing series of limited edition prints showing Nimbus (the character featured in my graphic novels) in unusual environments. These prints fulfill several passions of mine: my love for drawing architecture, my desire to work on a larger scale, and my never-ending search for the most wonderful inked brush line. I began this series in 2008 as a way of keeping the Professor Nimbus character alive in between lengthy graphic novel projects.

Otto Steininger

Carbon Footprint

On the occasion of a competition for a TV spot for the Alliance for Climate Protection, I teamed up with composer and sound effects specialist Brian Ales and writer David Levy (who also did the voiceover) to develop an idea. We brainstormed the subject and whittled down various approaches to this lighthearted and visually funny idea of a cartoony carbon footprint monster that gets tamed to the point of treading lightly. One friend of mine showed the clip to his three-year-old son, who proceeded to endlessly reenact it by stomping around the house in his father's shoes. For the execution of the animation in Flash, I drew on the help of two very talented young artists: Jasmina Mathieu and Hak Sue Kim.

JILLIAN TAMAKI
The Lynching of Louie Sam

These pieces accompanied an article in *The Walrus Magazine* that recounted the 1884 lynching of Louie Sam, a First Nations teenager who had been accused of murder. The vigilante mob disguised their identities by wearing face-paint, wrapping sheets around their heads, and wearing their wives' skirts. The illustrations capture the moment before the mob sets off to find Sam, who is represented by the riderless horse.

JILLIAN TAMAKI

Remembering Nana on Mother's Day

Mariko Tamaki (my cousin) and I created this Mother's Day piece for *The New York Times*'s Op-Art section. Nana (her given name), our father's mother, died before I was born and when Mariko was a small child. It is a family tradition for the Toronto wing of our family to visit Nana's grave on Mother's Day, then convene for a feast. The food is distinctly Japanese-Canadian—a strange mix of Japanese and Western food: Jell-O squares, sushi rolls, inari (referred to as "bags" by our family), chow mein, chicken wings, and fish cakes.

FRANK STOCKTON

A Shot at Glory

JEFFREY STEWART TIMMINS
The Long Journey Home

The Long Journey Home is a fable written by filmmaker Billie Mintz and inspired by the plight of a ten-year-old cancer patient, about whom Mintz made a documentary. The artwork was made with ink and watercolor, and individual elements were set up within a 3D space in Adobe After Effects. Each element was illustrated with the same tonal range, and atmospheric perspective was achieved by altering contrast, saturation, hue, and tone, relative to the elements' proximity to the "camera." Characters were built like paper dolls, with body parts layered on top of each other and hinged together. These characters were animated separately from the backgrounds, and nested into the scenes.

FRANCIS VALLEJO
The Advantages of Theodore Peeps

When Michael Meier and Nic Klein contacted me to contribute a short story to their *Dolor* anthology I was very excited. Having grown up on comic books, I was elated to be given the opportunity to create one of my own. The most challenging aspect was figuring out a story. I decided to use use a lyrical, almost Dr. Suess-ish, storytelling structure. Inspiration for the script came to me while I was going to bed. I live by myself in an old two-story Florida house so it's easy to let my imagination run wild. I vividly remember that as a child I threw the sheets over my head the moment I heard any kind of sinister sound in my room. So, the idea for the lyrics/script was born in a flurry in the middle of the night. The panels all came from childhood memories that have stuck with me to this day.

Kate T. Williamson

At a Crossroads: Between a Rock and My Parents' Place

These pieces are from a 144-page graphic memoir I wrote and illustrated about a three-month, post-college stopover at my parents' house in Pennsylvania that turned into a 23-month extended stay. Using comic book-style panels and full-page spreads, I depict highlights—attending a Hall & Oates concert with my mother on my birthday, my cousin's Renaissance-themed wedding, as well as low points and everyday moments—listening to cicadas on the roof, watching squirrels from my window. I wanted the images to be either detailed and funny or quiet and contemplative.

I began to look forward to seeing the squirrels each morning.

autumn ... again

TED WRIGHT

Let It Snow-Series

I was asked to do four illustrations that would be used in a holiday mailing for a real estate development in Canada named Ambleside. Nestled in a rural countryside with many trees and rolling hills, the area gets a tremendous amount of snow each year. For inspiration, art director Jeff

McLean asked me to listen to track #5 on the CD titled *A Charlie Brown Christmas*. The song title is *Christmas Time Is Here* and is an instrumental piano piece performed by Vince Guaraldi. It also happens to be my very favorite holiday song—I think it's simply beautiful.

STUDENT SCHOLARSHIP
AND
DISTINGUISHED EDUCATORS IN THE ARTS

The Society of Illustrators fulfills its education mission through its museum exhibitions, library, archives, permanent collection, and, most proudly, through the Student Scholarship Competition.

The following pages present a sampling of the 144 works selected from over 5,500 entries submitted by college-level students nationwide. The selections were made by a prestigious jury of professional illustrators.

Scott Bakal chairs this program and major financial support is given by the Society of Illustrators as well as various other generous private and corporate donors, including Dick Blick Artists Materials, the Illustration Academy, the Master Class Program, the late Arthur Zankel and other bequests established in memory of family and colleagues.

An endowment from bequests and corporate support makes possible over $60,000 in awards to the students.

Distinguished Educators in the Arts is an annual award selected by a nationwide jury of over 75 illustrators, art directors, and educators.

JOYCE ROGERS KITCHELL

[1945 – 2008]

The Society of Illustrators is dedicated to preserving the memory of Joyce Rogers Kitchell, a nationally reknowned watercolorist whose illustrations were sought for both private collections and commercial advertising.

We are committed to honoring her legacy and fostering her spirit of kindness and generosity.

Illustration by Joyce Rogers Kitchell, 1989

JAKE PANIAN

[SAN JOSE STATE UNIVERSITY]

2009 JURY: Anne Catharine Blake, Joe Ciardiello, Jordin Isip, Murray Tinkelman, and Soojin Buzelli.

RIGHT: Jake Panian and Judy Francis Zankel

Jake Panian.
Rattington, Photoshop.

The Society of Illustrators proudly presents the Zankel Scholar named in memory of Arthur Zankel, whose generous bequest has made this scholarship possible. Mr. Zankel was a firm advocate for higher education. This is the third year the Society has been honored to seek, in his name, the best of the junior class and to financially support his or her senior year of college.

The Zankel Scholar nominees from left to right: Katie Turner from Parsons the New School for Design, Kaeleen Wescoat-O'Neill from Art Center College of Design, Rebecca Stadtlander from Maryland Institute College of Art, and Jake Panian from San Jose State University.

TOM SGOUROS

Tom Sgouros talks to me all the time, and he doesn't even know it. I was a student at the Rhode Island School of Design, and it is his voice I recall most often when I am working now. What he had to say—about the history of illustration, editorial illustration, studio drawing, or my independent study—was always illuminating and funny. His words have been touchstones I return to again and again.

In studio drawing, he would give us a semester-long assignment to work on between classes. We were to take one object and draw it over and over for the entire 12 weeks. He wanted to see "mountains" of drawings. Well, it didn't take long for us to reach the "I have to draw this again?" stage. But that was when it got interesting. We had to push beyond the obvious and find new ways to approach that object on the page—to look beyond the object itself and really explore composition and design within the rectangle of the paper.

Tom's enthusiasm about the process of art is contagious. When I recall what he said, it's not just his words I hear, but also the quality of his voice. As much now as when I was a student, that excitement makes me want to get to work.

DAVID WIESNER

In 1965, all sophomore architecture students at RISD were required to take drawing. It was a transforming experience for me and may very well have sown the seeds that would eventually lead me away from that noble profession and into the world of illustration and books. I'm not saying any drawing course would have had such a life altering effect, but I was lucky enough to find myself in one of Tom Sgouros' classes. The primary focus was on drawing the figure. Anyone familiar with my handling of the human form in my early books will quickly surmise that I spent as little time as possible in front of a model. I was, with Tom's blessing, under a bridge somewhere or on one of Providence's many street corners drawing another landscape. What mattered to Tom was that we were engaged enough by whatever was in front of us so that we would actually think about marks we were making and their placement on the paper. To encourage us further, Tom would drag in prints of drawings by Degas, etchings by Pyranesi, and photographs of Cartier Bresson, among others.

Because of their wit, wisdom, and eloquence, I remember many of Tom's words, which is a good thing since I probably couldn't fully appreciate them at the time. The insight he offered verbally has been continually reinforced by the integrity of his example. As Tom gradually moved away from illustration and into painting, his determination to maintain the highest level of accomplishment in spite of the cruel assault of macular degeneration, has simply added to that resonant wisdom a profound inspiration.

DAVID MACAULAY

THOMAS FOGARTY

[1873 – 1938]

Now two generations past, Fogarty's work captured the core values of an American Society bookended by world war and economic depression. There is no greater example of this than in his illustration of Jacob August Riis' *Making of an American*, or *Sailing Alone Around the World*, Captain Joshua Slocum's account of his solo circumnavigation of the world aboard his 40–foot Spray, or his lifelong friendship and illustrative collaboration with Pulitzer Prize winner Ray Stannard Baker's alter ego, David Grayson. Fogarty was a prolific master having provided countless illustrations in not only some of the most popular books of the period but also in periodicals still popular today including *Harper's*, *Ladies Home Journal* and *Good Housekeeping*.

In the great tradition of instructors at the Art Students League, Fogarty stands among the greatest. While not a seeker of publicity, Fogarty quietly but firmly encouraged his students to seek avenues where they would find their greatest success. His impact on this nation's illustrative culture extends in the work of his students. As with many great instructors, Fogarty often placed his responsibility to his students above that of his own ambitions to ensure an ongoing and predestined value in the work of the next generation. When we think of Fogarty the teacher, we simply have to ask ourselves; where would our images of Southern gentility be without Walter Biggs? Where would the great depictions the Pa-

cific Naval Fleet have been without McClelland Barclay or for that matter, where would we be as a nation without Norman Rockwell? Never in the history of American Illustration was there a time when the great illustrative masters fanned the flames of great illustrative talent. His teaching as in his work was as much valued for its artisanship as it was for the cultural values that it instilled.

While a native of New York City, Fogarty was also part of the great tradition of artists who spent summers working in the finger lakes of New York capturing the elegant simplicity of life in Bristol Springs and Naples on Lake Canandaigua. Many summers were spent working in his studio adjacent to the family's beloved summer cottage, the Wigwam, where he created many of his most famous images in oil and pen and ink. In the fall, the family would return to New York City for him to continue his teaching at The League and his work for many of the most renowned publishing houses of the time.

In 1938, Fogarty died but not before passing his great talent onto his two sons Alexander, a composer, and Thomas, Jr. who followed in his father's footsteps to become one of the most beloved instructors at the Art Students League and a great American impressionist of his day.

TOM FOGARTY

FRANK REILLY

[1906 – 1967]

A newspaper columnist once wrote, "Frank Reilly is the greatest art teacher in the country." Wherever he was teaching, Mr. Reilly's classes were so popular, they filled to beyond capacity. With the model completely obscured, students in back rows drew and painted from easels in the line directly ahead of them. His ability to thoroughly present concept, technique, and procedure, were both legendary and instrumental to his success as a teacher. It was once related that, "Mr. Reilly could lecture for six hours on how to paint a bubble in a glass of beer."

However, the ability to inspire is truly a gift. In this regard, Frank Reilly's unselfishness is unparalleled. Although he enjoyed a distinguished career as an illustrator and innovator of artists materials, it is possible that the most important part of his life was teaching. Mr. Reilly could easily be considered one of the most influential artists of the twentieth century, so impressive is the roster of his former students.

Born in the heart of New York City, Frank J. Reilly, was the son of a Broadway actor and stage manager. This early exposure to the value of rehearsal and preparation undoubtedly had a lasting impression on the young Frank Reilly. Years later, as a pupil of Art Students League co-founder, Frank Vincent DuMond, Reilly would carefully chart and record his instructor's every brush stroke. He studied for a year and a half with DuMond, and another three with renowned anatomist, George Bridgeman.

As Bridgeman's successor at the ASL, Frank Reilly taught drawing, painting, picture making, and color abstraction. He was a meticulous perfectionist, who quickly became associated with success. Reilly witnessed the passing years of the Golden Age of Illustration Art, but recognized that there was an even larger landscape of assignments for well trained artists that were prepared to work hard and approach art as a profession. In this regard, his success was nothing less than monumental.

KENT STEINE

DADU DAVID SHIN
RUNNER
Mixed media
Rhode Island School of Design
Fred Lynch, Instructor
$5000 In Memory of Joyce Rogers Kitchell

BECCA GREEN
TOWER OF LEARNING
Oil
Kendall College of Art and Design
Jon McDonald, Instructor
$5000 In Memory of Arthur Zankel
2010 Call for Entries Poster

LEONARD DENTE
MAN IN HAT
Massachusetts College of Art and Design
Wojciech Wokynski, Instructor
$4000 Society of Illustrators
Education Committee Award

ARROLYN WEIDERHOLD
UNTITLED
Ringling College of Art and Design
Regan Dunnick, Instructor
$3000 In Memory of Albert Dorne
1 Week Illustration Academy Program

HAILEY KIM
THEY WILL SURVIVE V
Watercolor
Rhode Island School of Design
Jason Brockert, Instructor
$3000 In Memory of Barbara Bradley
7 Week Illustration Academy Program

FRANCIS VALLEJO
NASIR
Ringling College of Art and Design
George Pratt, Instructor
$2500 Society of Illustrators
Membership Committee Award

HOUSTON TRUEBLOOD
PINTORES E POLITICOS
Acrylic
Brigham Young University
Richard Hull, Instructor
$2500 Society of Illustrators
Achievement Award

IAN VANDERHILL
SOUND THE ALARM!
Digital montage
Grand Valley State University
Ed Wong-Lidga, Instructor
$2500 Microvisions Award

TORY NOVIKOVA
PETER AND THE WOLF
Pratt Institute
Lynne Foster, Instructor
$2000 Microvisions Award

James KC Ng
IMPERIAL AIRSHIP
Pencil and digital
School of Visual Arts
Stanley Martucci, Instructor
$2000 In Memory of Warren Rogers

Andrew Silver
SLEEP PARALYSIS
Digital
School of Visual Arts
Sal Catalano, Instructor
$2000 In Memory of Verdon Flory

Cassandra Piedra
SLEEPING BEAUTY
Ringling College of Art and Design
Mike Hodges, Instructor
$2000 In Memory of Richard Ely

CANNADY CHAPMAN
DON'T TRIP ME I SAY!
School of Visual Arts
Steve Brodner, Instructor
$1500 Alvin and Norma Pimsler Award

SARAH WURM
VEGGIE MONSTER
3D Mixed media
Columbus College of Art and Design
Mark Hazlerig, Instructor
$1500 In Honor of Barbara Carr

TSZ YAN CHEUNG
ARGON
Mixed media
San Jose State University
Alice Carter, Instructor
$1500 In Memory of
Helen Wohlberg Lambert
and Herman Lambert

MATT KOHR
NATURAL GRUNGE
Corel Painter
Savannah College of Art and Design
John Foerster, Instructor
$1000 Dan Adel Award

MATT BUCK
LOVECRAFT
Ringling College of Art and Design
Octavio Perez, Instructor
$1000 In Memory of Lila Dryer

KAT CIMINO
FAUST POSTER
Collage Savannah College of
Art and Design, Atlanta
Julie Mueller-Brown, Instructor
$1000 In Memory of
Joan M. McQuade

BILL NORRBY
LAST MAN ON EARTH
Oil on board
School of Visual Arts
Donato Giancola, Instructor
$1000 In Memory of Lila Dryer

EIKA YOKOYAMA
STAIRWELL – PORT 29
School of Visual Arts
Frances Jetter, Instructor
$1000 In Memory of Effie Bowie

Index

STEVE ADAMS
10109 Galeries d'Anjou Blvd.
Montreal H1J 2YA, Canada
514-352-6665
steve@adamillustration.com
www.adamillustration.com

P. 301
ART DIRECTORS: Bruno
Ricca, Renaud Plante
CLIENT: Les 400
Coups Publisher
MEDIUM: Acrylic,
digital

DANIEL ADEL
292 Main St.
Cold Spring, NY 10516
646-250-3206
danieladel@mindspring.com
www.danieladel.com

SILVER
P. 44
ART DIRECTOR:
David Harris
CLIENT: Vanity Fair
MEDIUM: Oil on
canvas

P. 46
ART DIRECTOR:
David Harris
CLIENT: Vanity Fair
MEDIUM: Oil

MONIKA AICHELE
Strassburgerstr. 10
Berlin 10405, Germany
+1-212-496-3706
mail@monikaaichele.com
www.monikaaichele.com

P. 145
ART DIRECTOR:
Fred Muenzmaier
CLIENT: Deautsche
Grammophon GMBH
MEDIUM: Mixed media

P. 464
ART DIRECTORS:
Stefan Sagmeister,
Alisa MacKenzie
CLIENT: Six Cities
Design Festival,
Scotland
MEDIUM: 3D

TAKASHI AKIYAMA
3-14-35 shimo-ochai
Shinjuku-ku
Tokyo 161-003, Japan
akiyama@t3.rim.or.jp

P. 234
ART DIRECTOR:
Takashi Akiyama
CLIENT: Tama Art
University
MEDIUM: Digital

P. 235
ART DIRECTOR:
Takashi Akiyama
CLIENT: Tama Art
University

KELLY ALDER
3306 Gloucester Rd.
Richmond, VA 23227
804-353-3113
kalder@comcast.net

P. 146
ART DIRECTORS:
Jessica Kantor,
Kelly Alder
CLIENT: Popidiot
MEDIUM: Crow-quill
pen, ink, computer

A. RICHARD ALLEN
31 Ridley Rd.
Bournemouth BH9 1LD, England
44-120-252-5181
info@arichardallen.com

P. 429
MEDIUM: Pencil,
acrylic, digital

WESLEY ALLSBROOK
99 Franklin St. #2L
Brooklyn, NY 11222
401-256-0255
wallsbroo@gmail.com

P. 465
ART DIRECTORS:
Liz Gorinsk,
Gina Gagliano
CLIENT: TOR
MEDIUM: Ink

PATRICK ARRASMITH
162 16th St. #8E
Brooklyn, NY 11215
718-499-4101
patrickarrasmith@earthlink.net
www.patrickarrasmith.com

P. 147
ART DIRECTOR:
Jeff Vanausdall
CLIENT:
The Jackson Group
MEDIUM: Scratch-
board, digital

SARAH ATLEE
1616 NW 40th St.
Oklahoma City, OK 73118
405-708-2927
sarahatlee@gmail.com
www.sarahatlee.com

P. 302
ART DIRECTOR:
Sarah Atlee
MEDIUM: Ink, collage
on found fabrics

SCOTT BAKAL
P.O. Box 531
Central Islip, NY 11722-0531
631-647-7074
info@scottbakal.com
www.scottbakal.com

P. 236
ART DIRECTORS:
Julia Breckenreid,
Scott Bakal
CLIENT: ICON5: New
York Real & Imagined
MEDIUM: Watercolor,
ink, acrylic

P. 430
MEDIUM: Acrylic

ANNA AND ELENA BALBUSSO
via Ciro Menotti 15
Milano 20129, Italy
0039-027-010-8739
balbusso.twins@gmail.com

P. 303
ART DIRECTOR:
Nadia Maestri
CLIENT: Black Cat
Publishing
MEDIUM: Acrylic,
digital

P. 304
ART DIRECTOR:
Elisabeth Cohat
CLIENT:
Gallimard Jeunesse
MEDIUM: Acrylic,
digital

P. 305
ART DIRECTOR:
Elisabeth Cohat
CLIENT:
Gallimard Jeunesse
MEDIUM: Acrylic,
digital

P. 306
ART DIRECTOR:
Elisabeth Cohat
CLIENT:
Gallimard Jeunesse
MEDIUM: Acrylic,
digital

P. 307
ART DIRECTOR:
Nadia Maestri
CLIENT: Black Cat
Publishing
MEDIUM: Acrylic,
digital

ANDREW BANNECKER
7131 Arlington Rd. #222
Bethesda, MD 20814
917-209-3462
abannecker@gmail.com
www.andrewbannecker.com

P. 431
MEDIUM: Digital

ISTVAN BANYAI
PO Box 329
Lakeville, CT 06039
860-435-2940
ibanyai@sbcglobal.net
www.ist-one.com

P. 47
ART DIRECTOR:
Brian Anstey
CLIENT:
Entertainment Weekly
MEDIUM: Ink, collage,
digital

ANGELA BARBALACE
135 Chapman Ave.
Hamilton, NJ 08610
609-585-1259
abarbalace@artspan.com

P. 308
ART DIRECTOR:
Rachel Rubin Wolf
CLIENT: Splash 10
MEDIUM: Watercolor

MICHAEL BARTALOS

P. 237
ART DIRECTOR:
Richard Sheaff
CLIENT:
US Postal Service
MEDIUM: Digital

KENT BARTON
c/o Richard Solomon Artists Rep
149 Madison Ave. #708
New York, NY 10016
212-223-9545
richard@richardsolomon.com
www.richardsolomon.com

P. 466
ART DIRECTORS:
Kemberly Wilder,
Shayne Millington
CLIENT: Oil of Olay
MEDIUM:
Scratchboard

MELINDA BECK
536 5th St. #2
Brooklyn, NY 11215
718-499-0985
studio@melindabeck.com
www.melindabeck.com

P. 48
ART DIRECTOR:
Lisa Nitzche
CLIENT:
Dogs Magazine

P. 238
ART DIRECTOR:
Ale Mercado
CLIENT: Kilkenny
County Council

P. 239
CLIENT: Threadbare
MEDIUM: Silkscreen

JUSTINE BECKETT
c/o Frank Sturges
142 W Winter St.
Delaware, OH 43015
740-369-9702
frank@sturgesreps.com
www.sturgesreps.com

P. 240
ART DIRECTOR:
Steve Gabor
CLIENT: Baseman
Printing, Salvator Coe
& Gabor
MEDIUM: Digital

LINDA FENNIMORE
808 W End Ave. #801
New York, NY 10025
lzfennimore@verizon.net

P. 172
CLIENT: Raptor Trust,
Millington NJ
MEDIUM: Watercolor

P. 182
ART DIRECTOR:
Frank Verlizzo
CLIENT: Bill Haber
MEDIUM:
Colored pencil

JEFFREY FISHER
c/o Riley Illustration
PO Box 92
New Paltz, NY 12561
845-255-3309
teresa@rileyillustration.com
www.rileyillustration.com

P. 173
ART DIRECTOR:
Susan Feery
CLIENT: TravelSmith
MEDIUM: Acrylic

BART J. FORBES
3017 Green Hill Dr.
Plano, TX 75093
972-306-9753
bart@bartforbes.com
www.bartforbes.com

P. 252
ART DIRECTOR:
Cheryl Vogel
CLIENT: Valley House
MEDIUM:
Oil on board

JON FOSTER
118 Everett Ave.
Providence, RI 02906
401-277-0880
alpine117@verizon.net

P. 331
ART DIRECTOR:
Chris Stengel
CLIENT: Scholastic
MEDIUM: Digital

P. 332
ART DIRECTOR:
Bill Schafer
CLIENT:
Subterranean Press
MEDIUM: Digital

P. 333

ALEXANDRA FRANK
2770 Sacramento St.
San Francisco, CA 94115
650-207-1936
alexandra.frank@gmail.com
P. 334
MEDIUM: Watercolor,
gouache, pencil

DOUGLAS FRASER
Bridge Graphics
1161 Camrose Crescent
Victoria, British Columbia,V8P 1M9,
Canada
250-385-4881
doug@fraserart.com
www.fraserart.com

P. 174
ART DIRECTOR:
Travis McElhany
CLIENT: VML Inc.
MEDIUM:
Alkyds, digital color

MARK FREDRICKSON
56340 Bear Lake Rd.
Hancock, MI 49930
906-483-0776
fredricksonart@cox.net

P. 335
ART DIRECTOR:
Daniel Kinski
CLIENT: Daniel Kinski
MEDIUM: Digital

THOMAS FUCHS
320 W 37th St. #9D
New York, NY 10018
212-904-1255
mail@thomasfuchs.com
www.thomasfuchs.com

P. 77
ART DIRECTOR:
Ashley Bond
CLIENT: Pluto Media
MEDIUM: Acrylic

YOKO FURUSHO
265 1st Ave. #5
New York, NY 10003
917-501-1247
info@yokofurusho.com
www.yokofurusho.com

P. 175
ART DIRECTOR:
Mike Worthington
CLIENT: Plushgun
MEDIUM: Ink, acrylic

NICK GAETANO
nic1@cox.net

P. 176
ART DIRECTOR:
Jeanette Aramburu
CLIENT: Gallo
MEDIUM:
Acrylic on canvas

CHRIS GALL
4421 N Camino del Santo
Tucson, AZ 85718
520-299-4454
chris@chrisgall.com
www.chrisgall.com

P. 177
ART DIRECTOR:
Jim Burke
CLIENT:
Della Graphics
MEDIUM:
Scratchboard/CS2

P. 253
ART DIRECTOR:
Clay Turner
CLIENT:
Natural Gas Institute
MEDIUM:
Scratchboard/CS2

DENISE GALLAGHER
130 Meadow Glen
Youngsville, LA 70592
337-412-2326
denise@denisegallagher.com
www.denisegallagher.com

P. 336
ART DIRECTOR:
Denise Gallagher
CLIENT: Von Glitschka
MEDIUM:
Graphite, digital

BEPPE GIACOBBE
c/o Morgan Gaynin Inc.
194 Third Avenue #3
New York, NY 10003
212.475.0440
info@morgangaynin.com
www.morgangaynin.com

P. 337
CLIENT:
Editions du Rouergue
MEDIUM: Digital

DONATO GIANCOLA
397 Pacific St.
Brooklyn, NY 11217
718-797-2438
donato@donatoart.com
www.donatoart.com

P. 340
ART DIRECTOR:
Irene Gallo
CLIENT: Tor Books
MEDIUM: Oil on panel

BEN GIBSON
911 Union St. #3
Brooklyn, NY 11215
646-335-5962
ben@ben-gibson.com
www.ben-gibson.com

P. 338
ART DIRECTOR:
Sean McDonald
CLIENT:
Riverhead Books
MEDIUM:
Mixed, digital

P. 339
ART DIRECTOR:
Angela Carlino
CLIENT:
Random House
MEDIUM:
Mixed, digital

MICHAEL GLENWOOD
13908 Stonefield Ln.
Clifton, VA 20124
888-818-9811
mike@mglenwood.com
www.mglenwood.com

P. 84
ART DIRECTOR:
Jody Mustain
CLIENT: United Air-
lines/Hemispheres
Magazine
MEDIUM: Digital

P. 445
MEDIUM: Digital

VON GLITSCHKA
1976 Fitzpatrick Ave. SE
Salem, OR 97306
971-223-6143
von@glitschka.com
www.glitschka.com

P. 178
ART DIRECTOR:
Von Glitschka
CLIENT: Brian Ward
MEDIUM: Digital

RICHARD A. GOLDBERG
15 Cliff St.
Arlington, MA 02476-5907
781-258-7079
rag@ragmedia.com

P. 254
ART DIRECTOR:
Lisa Samar
CLIENT: Great Arrow
Greeting Card
MEDIUM: Pen & ink,
gouache, digital

P. 446
MEDIUM: Pen & ink,
gouache, digital

DAVID GORDON
305 Riverside Dr. #5D
New York, NY 10025
917-620-3089
daveygordon@mac.com

P. 341
ART DIRECTOR:
Mike Knapp
CLIENT:
Random House
MEDIUM: Photoshop

P. 342
ART DIRECTOR:
Heather Wood
CLIENT:
Penguin Putnam
MEDIUM: Photoshop

P. 343
ART DIRECTOR:
Heather Wood
CLIENT:
Penguin Putnam
MEDIUM: Photoshop

ALESSANDRO GOTTARDO
Arto Design
Via Stradella 13
Milan 20129, Italy
+39 335-704-9862
conceptualillustration@gmail.com

P. 80
ART DIRECTOR:
SooJin Buzelli
CLIENT: Plansponsor
MEDIUM: Digital

P. 81
ART DIRECTOR:
Giovanni De Mauro
MEDIUM: Digital

P. 179
ART DIRECTOR:
Antonella Bandoli
CLIENT: SEAC
MEDIUM: Digital

P. 260
ART DIRECTOR:
Laurel Yankovich
CLIENT: Harrah's

P. 261
ART DIRECTOR:
Laurel Yankovich
CLIENT: Harrah's
MEDIUM: Acrylic

P. 262
ART DIRECTOR:
Laurel Yankovich
CLIENT: Harrah's
MEDIUM:
Acrylic on board

P. 482
ART DIRECTOR:
David Harris
CLIENT: Vanity Fair

JASON HOLLEY
391 W Grandview Ave.
Sierra Madre, CA 91024
626-836-7700
harpy23@sprintmail.com

P. 85
ART DIRECTOR:
Kory Kennedy
CLIENT:
Runner's World

JEREMY HOLMES
Mutt Ink
616 Roberts Ave.
Glenside, PA 19038
215-533-6971
jholmes@muttink.com
jholmes@muttink.com

P. 354
ART DIRECTOR:
Cindy McFarland
CLIENT:
Storey Publishing
MEDIUM: Mixed

PAUL HOPPE
212 Monitor St.
Brooklyn, NY 11222
917-774-5455
info@paulhoppe.com
www.paulhoppe.com

P. 183
ART DIRECTORS:
Christopher Karl,
Lars Harmsen
CLIENT: Finest/Magma
Brand Communica-
tion Group
MEDIUM: Pen, brush
& ink, digital

STERLING HUNDLEY
14361 Old Bond St.
Chesterfield, VA 23832
804-306-9536
sterling@sterlinghundley.com
www.sterlinghundley.com

P. 89
ART DIRECTOR:
Tyler Darden
CLIENT: Virginia
Living Magazine
MEDIUM: Acrylic, ink,
gouache on board

P. 186
ART DIRECTOR:
Cathleen Tefft
CLIENT: Arena Stage
MEDIUM: Gouache,
acrylic, ink

MIRKO ILIC
207 E 32nd St.
New York, NY 10016
212-481-9737
studio@mirkoilic.com
www.mirkoilic.com

P. 90
ART DIRECTOR:
Tim Luddy
CLIENT: Mother Jones
MEDIUM:
Maya, Photoshop

P. 91
ART DIRECTOR: Rob
Wilson
CLIENT: Playboy

RYAN INZANA
114 Clinton St.
Lambertville, NJ 08530
609-397-4823
rinzana@aol.com

P. 483
EDITOR: Peter Kuper
CLIENT: World
War 3 Illustrated
MEDIUM: Ink on
paper, Photoshop

JORDIN ISIP
536 5th St
Brooklyn, NY 11215
718-499-0985
jordin@jordinisip.com
www.jordinisip.com

P. 263
ART DIRECTOR:
Rich Jacobs
CLIENT: Virgin Mobile
MEDIUM:
Mixed on panel

MARIKO JESSE
21 Dunsfold Rise
Coulsdon, Greater London CR5 2ED,
England
(44) 020-8660-0120
mariko@jesse@usa.net
www.marikojesse.com

P. 92
ART DIRECTOR:
Jowie Chan
CLIENT:
Muse Magazine
MEDIUM: Etching

FRANCES JETTER
390 West End Ave.
New York, NY 10024
212-580-3720
fjetter@earthlink.net
www.francesjetter.com

P. 264
ART DIRECTOR:
Stephen Fredericks
CLIENT: The New York
Society of Etchers
MEDIUM: Linocut

JOHN KACHIK
747 Rustling Leaf Ct.
Sykesville, MD 21784
410-552-1900
kachikart@comcast.net

P. 187
ART DIRECTOR:
Carol Ross
CLIENT: Tom and
Sally's Homemade
Chocolates
MEDIUM:
Mixed, Photoshop

P. 355
ART DIRECTOR:
Karen Nelson
CLIENT:
Sterling Publishing
MEDIUM:
Mixed, Photoshop

JAMES KACZMAN
123 Elm St.
Stonington, CT 06378
860-535-9091
jameskaczman@comcast.net

P. 356
ART DIRECTOR:
Scott Magoon
CLIENT: Houghton
Mifflin Publishing
Company
MEDIUM: Acrylic

GWENDA KACZOR
c/o Marlena Agency
322 Ewing St.
Princeton, NJ 08540
609.252.9405
marlena@marlenaagency.com
www.marlenaagency.com

P. 188
ART DIRECTOR:
Peter Prandato
CLIENT:
Coldwater Creek
MEDIUM: Digital

P. 265
ART DIRECTOR:
Julia Breckenreid
CLIENT: ICON5
MEDIUM: Digital

AYA KAKEDA
712 Manhattan Ave. #2
Brooklyn, NY 11222
646-526-6857
aya@ayakakeda.com
www.ayakakeda.com

P. 357
ART DIRECTOR:
Jacob Covey
CLIENT: Fantagraphics
MEDIUM:
Silkscreen, charcoal

P. 484
ART DIRECTOR:
Chris Butzer
CLIENT: Rabbitrab-
bit@comic.com

SATOSHI KAMBAYASHI
40 Tisbury Rd., Flat 2
Hove BN3 3BA, England
44-127-377-1539
satoshi.k@virgin.net

P. 93
ART DIRECTOR:
Roger Browning
CLIENT: The Guardian
MEDIUM: Digital

GARY KELLEY
c/o Richard Solomon Artists Rep
149 Madison Ave. #708
New York, NY 10016
212-223-9545
scott@richardsolomon.com
ww.richardsolomon.com

P. 358
ART DIRECTOR:
Rita Marshall
CLIENT:
Creative Editions
MEDIUM: Pastel

P. 359
ART DIRECTOR:
Rita Marshall
CLIENT:
Creative Editions
MEDIUM: pastel

P. 360
ART DIRECTOR:
Rita Marshall
CLIENT:
Creative Editions
MEDIUM: Pastel

SEAN KELLY
126 Jackman Ave.
Fairfield, CT 06825
203-615-0118
sean@seankellystudio.com
www.seankellystudio.com

P. 98
ART DIRECTOR:
Michael Kolomatsky
CLIENT:
The New York Times
MEDIUM:
Pencil, ink wash

SOOSA KIM
655673-1567 Tennessee #106
San Francisco, CA 94107

P. 266
CLIENT:
Totoro Forest Project
MEDIUM: Oil

LORENZO MATTOTTI
www.mattotti.com

P. 101
ART DIRECTOR OF COVERS:
Françoise Mouly
CLIENT:
The New Yorker

BILL MAYER
240 Forkner Dr.
Decatur, GA 30030
404-378-0686
bill@thebillmayer.com
www.thebillmayer.com

P. 191
ART DIRECTOR:
Joe Albert
CLIENT:
Grey Advertising
MEDIUM: Pen, digital

P. 192
ART DIRECTOR:
Matthew Willis
CLIENT:
Blueprint Partners
MEDIUM: Airbrush,
gouache, digital

P. 193
ART DIRECTOR:
Matthew Willis
CLIENT:
Blueprint Partners
MEDIUM: Airbrush,
gouache, digital

P. 271
ART DIRECTOR:
Joe Albert
CLIENT:
Grey Advertising
MEDIUM: Pen, digital

P. 370
ART DIRECTOR:
Tom Eigner
CLIENT: Avon Books
MEDIUM: Airbrush,
gouache, digital

HAL MAYFORTH
145 Deronde Rd.
Montpelier, VT 05602
802-229-2716
may4th@pshift.com
www.mayforth.com

SILVER
P. 427
MEDIUM: Acrylic on
wood panel

P. 452
MEDIUM: Acrylic on
wood panel

ADAM MCCAULEY
1081 Treat Ave.
San Francisco, CA 94110
415-826-5668
adam@adammccauley.com
www.adammccauley.com

P. 272
ART DIRECTOR:
Ronn Campisi
CLIENT:
The Boston College
MEDIUM:
Scratchboard, digital

GOLD
P. 296
ART DIRECTORS:
Cynthia Wigginton,
Scott Piehl
CLIENT:
Sterling Publishers
MEDIUM:
Scratchboard, digital

P. 378
ART DIRECTOR:
Rebecca Morrison
CLIENT:
Random House UK
MEDIUM:
Scratchboard, liquid
acrylic, colored pencil

GRADY MCFERRIN
141 Noble St. #3
Brooklyn, NY 11222
917-495-7268
grady@gmillustration.com
www.gmillustration.com

P. 194
ART DIRECTOR:
Carson Ellis
MEDIUM: Digital

ROBERT MEGANCK
Communication Design
2201 W Broad St. #108
Richmond, VA 23220-2022
804-594-0850
robert@meganck.com
www.meganck.com

P. 196
ART DIRECTORS:
Laura Chessin,
Sage Brown
CLIENT: Sheryl Warner
and the Southside
Homewreckers
MEDIUM: Digital

P. 197
ART DIRECTOR:
Bruce Miller
CLIENT:
Barksdale Theatre
MEDIUM: Digital

LUC MELANSON
71, Avenue Parissi
Laval, Quebec H7N 3S4, Canada
450-975-7836
luc@lucmelanson.com
www.lucmelanson.com

P. 376
ART DIRECTOR:
Janine Vangool
CLIENT:
Vangool Design
MEDIUM: Mixed

P. 377
ART DIRECTOR:
Cecile Petit
CLIENT: Milan/
Groundwood Books
MEDIUM: Digital

P. 450
MEDIUM: Mixed

P. 451
MEDIUM: Mixed

AARON MESHON
232 President St. #2L
Brooklyn, NY 11231
718-858-8485
hello@aaronmeshon.com

P. 195
ART DIRECTOR:
Willy Wong
CLIENT:
NY and Company
MEDIUM: Acrylic

RENÉ MILOT
49 Thorncliffe Pk Dr. #1604
Toronto, Ontario M4H 1J6, Canada
416-425-7726
renemilot@renemilot.com
www.renemilot.com

P. 198
ART DIRECTOR:
Jonathan Nicol
CLIENT:
Cirque du Soleil
MEDIUM: Digital

P. 489
ART DIRECTOR:
Jonathan Nicol
CLIENT:
Cirque du Soleil
MEDIUM: Digital

WENDELL MINOR
PO Box 1135
15 Old North Rd.
Washington, CT 06793
860-868-9101
wendell@minorart.com
www.minorart.com

P. 371
ART DIRECTOR:
Martha Rago
CLIENT: HarperCollins
MEDIUM: Mixed

P. 372
ART DIRECTOR:
Laurent Linn
CLIENT: Henry Holt
MEDIUM: Mixed

P. 373
ART DIRECTOR:
Matthew Miller
CLIENT: Toby Press
MEDIUM: Mixed

P. 374
ART DIRECTOR:
Martha Rago
CLIENT: HarperCollins
MEDIUM: Mixed

P. 375
ART DIRECTOR:
John Fontana
CLIENT:
Nan Talese Books
MEDIUM: Mixed

PEP MONTSERRAT
c/o Marlena Agency
322 Ewing St.
Princeton, NJ 08540
609-252-9405
marlena@marlenaagency.com
www.marlenaagency.com

P. 379
ART DIRECTOR:
Debbie Sfetsios
CLIENT:
Simon & Schuster
MEDIUM: Digital

P. 380
ART DIRECTOR:
Noemi Mercade
CLIENT:
Combel Editorial
MEDIUM: Digital

P. 381
ART DIRECTOR:
Noemi Mercade
CLIENT:
Combel Editorial
MEDIUM: Digital

DOUG MOSS
401 E. 8th St. #304
Sioux Falls SD 57103
605-275-0011
dmoss@insightmarketingdesign.com
www.insightmarketingdesign.com

P. 392
ART DIRECTOR:
Doug Moss
CLIENT: Insight
Marketing Design
MEDIUM:
Pen & ink, computer

KEN ORVIDAS
16724 NE 138th Ct.
Woodinville, WA 98072
425-867-3072
ken@orvidas.com
www.orvidas.com

P. 274
ART DIRECTOR:
Winnie Hulm
CLIENT:
Jennifer Owen
MEDIUM: Digital

JOHN JUDE PALENCAR
3435 Hamlin Rd.
Medina, OH 44256
330-725-5292
ninestandingstones@yahoo.com
www.johnjudepalencar.com

P. 396
ART DIRECTOR:
Irene Gallo
CLIENT: Tor Books
MEDIUM: Acrylic

MICHAEL PARASKEVAS
157 Tuckahoe Ln.
Southampton, NY 11968
631-287-1665
jrkroll@mac.com

P. 208
ART DIRECTORS:
Shanette Barth
Cohen,
Rosanna Braccini
CLIENT: The Hampton
Classic Horse Show
MEDIUM: Acrylic

P. 209
ART DIRECTORS:
Shanette Barth
Cohen,
Rosanna Braccini
CLIENT: The Hampton
Classic Horse Show
MEDIUM: Acrylic

JAKE PARKER
14 Valleywood Rd.
Cos Cob, CT 06807
203-422-2022
jake@agent44.com

P. 492
ART DIRECTOR:
Jake Parker
CLIENT:
Out of Picture II
MEDIUM:
Pencil, digital

VALERIA PETRONE
Via Altaguardia 15
Milano 20135, Italy
39-02-583-0777-1
valeria@valeriapetrone.com
www.valeriapetrone.com

P. 210
ART DIRECTOR:
Bob Barrie
CLIENT:
United Airlines
MEDIUM: Digital

P. 275
ART DIRECTOR:
Cristiano Guerri
CLIENT: Feltrinelli
MEDIUM: Digital

EMMANUEL PIERRE
c/o Riley Illustration
PO Box 92
New Paltz, NY 12561
845-255-3309
info@rileyillustration.com
www.rileyillustration.com

P. 276
ART DIRECTOR:
Catherine Omen
MEDIUM: Collage

P. 277
ART DIRECTOR:
Lauren Stoskopff
MEDIUM: Collage

P. 397
CLIENT:
Martine Gossieaux
MEDIUM: Mixed

DAVID PLUNKERT
3504 Ash St.
Baltimore, MD 21211
410-235-7803
info@spurdesign.com
www.davidplunkert.com

P. 108
ART DIRECTOR:
Jennifer Carling
CLIENT:
Harvard Magazine
MEDIUM: Mixed

P. 109
ART DIRECTOR:
Aviva Michaelov
CLIENT:
The New York Times
MEDIUM: Mixed

BILL PLYMPTON
153 W 27th St. #1005
New York, NY 10001
212-741-0322
plymptoons@aol.com

P. 493
ART DIRECTOR:
Bill Plympton
CLIENT: Parson Brown
MEDIUM:
Pencil on paper

EMILIANO PONZI
c/o Magnet Reps
1685 H St. #219
Blaine, WA 98230
866-390-5656
art@magnetreps.com
www.magnetreps.com

SILVER
P. 45
ART DIRECTOR:
Nicholas Blechman
CLIENT:
The New York Times
MEDIUM: Digital

P. 110
ART DIRECTOR:
Joseph Caserto
CLIENT:
Business Week
MEDIUM: Digital

JOHN RABOU
Luybenstraat 13
's-Hertogenbosch 5211 BR,
The Netherlands
00-31-73-6137337
jrabou@tiscali.nl

P. 494
CLIENT: Carolien van
Loon, Tim de Ridder,
Town Archeologist
MEDIUM: Watercolor
on paper

CHRIS RAHN
1236 SE Harney #2
Portland, OR 97202
415-810-4662
chris@rahnart.com
www.rahnart.com

P. 111
ART DIRECTOR:
Derek Rainey
CLIENT: LA Weekly
MEDIUM: Digital

P. 398
ART DIRECTOR:
Sarah Olson
CLIENT: Academy
Chicago Publishers
MEDIUM: Oils

JAMES RANSOME
107 Knollwood Rd.
Rhinebeck, NY 12572
845-876-2148
jransomeillustr@aol.com

P. 399
ART DIRECTOR:
Rachael Cole
CLIENT: Schwart and
Wade Publishing
MEDIUM: Oil

ANDY RASH
298 Metropolitan Ave. #B4
Brooklyn, NY 11211
718-486-7820
mail@rashworks.com
www.rashworks.com

P. 400
ART DIRECTOR:
Donna Mark
CLIENT: Bloomsbury
Publishing
MEDIUM: Mixed

GUILLERMO REAL
111 South Broadway #2H
White Plains, NY 10605
707-548-0630
williereal@gmail.com

P. 495
ART DIRECTOR:
Guillermo Real
CLIENT: Out of Picture
MEDIUM:
Pen & ink, digital

THE RED NOSE STUDIO
c/o Magnet Reps
1685 H St. #219
Blaine, WA 98230
866-390-5656
art@magnetreps.com
www.magnetreps.com

P. 211
ART DIRECTOR:
David Plunkert
CLIENT: Serbin
Communications,
Directory of
Illustration
MEDIUM: 3D

P. 496
ART DIRECTOR:
May Wong
CLIENT: TIME
MEDIUM: 3D

P. 497
ART DIRECTORS:
Hans Martin,
Andre Koot
CLIENT: ASKO

ROBERT RENDO
60-10 47th Ave. #15G
Woodside, NY 11377
718-446-7861
artwork88@aol.com

P. 453
MEDIUM:
Pen & ink

PAOLO RIVERA
59 Scholes St. #102
Brooklyn, NY 11206
386-846-3802
paolo@paolorivera.com
www.paolorivera.com

P. 498
CLIENT:
Marvel Comics
MEDIUM:
Acrylic, gouache

EDEL RODRIGUEZ
16 Ridgewood Ave.
PO Box 102
Mt Tabor, NJ 07878
973-983-7776
edelrodriguez@aol.com

SILVER
P. 141
ART DIRECTOR:
Anthony Swaneveld
CLIENT:
Soulpepper Theatre
MEDIUM: Acrylic,
ink on paper

P. 212
ART DIRECTOR:
Anthony Swaneveld
CLIENT:
Soulpepper Theatre
MEDIUM: Acrylic,
ink on paper

P. 213
ART DIRECTORS:
Whitney Sherman,
David Plunkert
CLIENT: ICON5
MEDIUM: Mixed

P. 214
Art Director:
Anthony Swaneveld
Client:
Soulpepper Theatre
Medium: Acrylic, ink

P. 215
Art Director:
Client: Viacom
Medium: Mixed

SILVER
P. 299
Art Director:
Helen Yentus
Client:
Random House
Medium: Mixed

P. 402
Client: Farrar, Straus
and Giroux
Medium: Pastel, color
pencil on paper

P. 403
Client:
Velo Press
Medium:
Mixed

PAUL ROGERS
12 South Fair Oaks Ave. #208
Pasadena, CA 91105
626-564-8728
paulrogers@attglobal.net

P. 401
Art Director:
Jennifer Lee
Client:
American Express
Medium:
Ink, acrylic, digital

MARC ROSENTHAL
39 Cliffwood St.
Lenox, MA 01240
413-446-7831
vze2c9cu@verizon.net

P. 278
Art Director:
Michel Bohbot
Client: National
Labor Federation
Calendar
Medium: Ink, digital

GOLD
P. 460
Art Director:
Steven Guarnaccia
Client: Coesia
Medium: Ink, digital

THILO ROTHACKER
Moerikestrasse 24b
Stuttgart 70178, Germany
+49 (173) 341-1595
thilo@thilo-rothacker.com
www.thilo-rothacker.com

P. 112
Art Director:
Wolfgang Seidl
Client: Red Indians
Publishing,
Ramp Magazine
Medium: Digital

GRAHAM ROUMIEU
c/o Magnet Reps
1685 H St., #219
Blaine, WA 98230
866-390-5656
art@magnetreps.com
www.magnetreps.com

P. 113
Art Director:
Cinders McLeod
Client:
The Globe & Mail
Medium: Watercolor

P. 499
Editor: Emily Haynes
Client: Plume,
Penguin Group
Medium: Watercolor

JIM RUGG
113 Amherst Pl.
Glenshaw, PA 15116
412-213-0242
jimrugg@hotmail.com

P. 500
Art Directors:
Joe Keatings,
Mark Andrew Smith
Client: Erik Larsen
Medium:
Pen & ink, digital

JASON SADLER
47 Pleasant Ave.
White Plains, NY 10605
914-949-1877
jason_sadler@hotmail.com

P. 501
Art Director:
Jason Sadler
Client: Out of Picture
Medium: Digital,
Flash, Photoshop)

RACHEL SALOMON
61 Greenpoint Ave. #400
Brooklyn, NY 11222
718-637-1073
rachel@rachelsalomon.com
www.rachelsalomon.com

P. 404
Art Director:
Miriam Rosenbloom
Client: Faber
Medium: Acrylic, ink

RUTH SANDERSON
PO Box 285
Easthampton, MA 01027
413-529-1829
ruth@ruthsanderson.com
www.ruthsanderson.com

P. 405
Art Director:
Tracy Shaw
Client: Little, Brown
and Company
Medium:
Oils on panel

ZINA SAUNDERS
210 E 17 St. #6B
New York, NY 10003
212-777-1201
zina@zinasaunders.com
www.zinasaunders.com

P. 502
Client:
Arthur Magazine
Medium: Mixed

STEPHEN SAVAGE
93 Third Pl. #3
Brooklyn, NY 11231
917-843-1339
stephen.savage@earthlink.net
www.stephensavage.com

P. 114
Art Director:
Eric Capossela
Client:
Atlanta Magazine
Medium: Needlepoint

CHRIS SHEBAN
2861 Shannon Ct.
Northbrook, IL 60062-4379
847-412-9707
c.sheban@att.net
chrissheban.com

P. 279
Art Director:
Al Shackelford
Client:
Duluth Trading Co.
Medium: Watercolor,
color pencil

WHITNEY SHERMAN
5101 Whiteford Ave.
Baltimore, MD 21212
410-435-2095
ws@whitneysherman.com
www.whitneysherman.com

P. 280
Art Director:
Whitney Sherman
Client: The Urban
Forest Project/
Baltimore
Medium:
Graphite, digital

YUKO SHIMIZU
917-379-2636
yuko@yukoart.com
www.yukoart.com

P. 116
Art Director:
SooJin Buzelli
Client: Planspansor
Magazine
Medium: Ink drawing,
digital coloring

P. 117
Art Director:
Nicholas Blechman
Client: The New York
Times Book Review
Medium: Ink drawing,
digital coloring

P. 216
Client: TBWA Paris
Medium: Ink drawing,
digital coloring

P. 217
Art Director:
Andrew Cook
Client: Microsoft
Medium: Ink drawing,
digital coloring

P. 218
Art Director:
Andrew Cook
Client: Microsoft
Medium: Ink drawing,
digital coloring

P. 406
Art Directors:
Karen Berger,
Pornsak Pichetshote
Client: DC Vertigo
Medium: Ink drawing,
digital coloring

P. 407
Art Directors:
Karen Berger,
Pornsak Pichetshote
Client: DC Vertigo
Medium: Ink drawing,
digital coloring

P. 503
Art Directors:
Frank Blackwell,
Matt Collier,
Kylie McLean
Client: Tiger Beer,
CHI & Partners
Medium: Ink drawing,
digital coloring

SIMONE SHIN
PO Box 1084
South Pasadena, CA 91031
626-755-7420
sjaeshin@yahoo.com
www.simoneshin.com

GOLD
P. 424
Medium: Silkscreen
on paper

STEVE SIMPSON
21 Villarea Park
Glenageary, Ireland
353-087-265-9641
mail@stevesimpson.com
www.stevesimpson.com

P. 408
Art Director:
Henry Muldow
Client: Foundation
Cultural Dream-
weavers
Medium:
Pencil, digital

MICHAEL SLOAN
39 Linden St.
New Haven, CT 06511-2526
203-887-1243
michaelsloan@earthlink.net

P. 504
Medium: Giclee print

P. 281
Art Director:
Paola Vita
Client:
NYC Outward Bound
Medium: Brush & ink,
gouache, watercolor

OWEN SMITH
1608 Fernside Blvd.
Alameda, CA 94501
510-865-1911
owensmithart@att.net

P. 282
ART DIRECTOR:
Judy Moran
CLIENT: San Francisco
Arts Commission
MEDIUM:
Oil on board

P. 283
ART DIRECTOR:
Steve Brodner
CLIENT: Society of
Illustrators/Artists
Against the War
MEDIUM: Oil on board

OTTO STEININGER
144 W 27th St. #6F
New York, NY 10001
646-706-6229
steininger@mindspring.com
www.ottosteininger.com

P. 115
ART DIRECTOR:
Athena St. Jacques
CLIENT: Toronto Life
Magazine
MEDIUM: Digital

P. 505

FRANK STOCKTON
110 E 7th St. #11
New York, NY 10009
626-347-9707
frank@frankstockton.com
www.frankstockton.com

P. 118
ART DIRECTOR:
Russell Estes
CLIENT:
Intelligence Report
MEDIUM: Ink, digital

P. 409
ART DIRECTOR:
Jacob Covey
CLIENT: Fantagraphics
MEDIUM: Ink, digital

P. 508
ART DIRECTOR:
Siung Tjia
CLIENT: ESPN
The Magazine
MEDIUM: Ink, digital

DAVE STOLTE
32163 Cala Torrente
Temecula, CA 92592
949-378-5520
dave@davestolte.com
HTTP://www.davestolte.com

P. 284
CLIENT:
Stacy Masserchmidt,
Fraulein Affair Gallery
MEDIUM:
Pencil, digital

MARK STUTZMAN
Eloqui
100 G St.
Mt. Lake Park, MD 21550-3611
301-334-3994
mark@eloqui.com
www.eloqui.com

P. 220
ART DIRECTOR:
Mark Minter
CLIENT:
Palm Beach Opera
MEDIUM:
Watercolor, airbrush

P. 221
ART DIRECTOR:
Mark Minter
CLIENT:
Palm Beach Opera
MEDIUM:
Watercolor, airbrush

JILLIAN TAMAKI
268 Nassau Ave. #3L
Brooklyn, NY 11222
917-359-3693
jill@jilliantamaki.com
www.jilliantamaki.com

P. 119
ART DIRECTOR:
William Hooks
CLIENT:
Entertainment Weekly
MEDIUM: Ink, digital

P. 120
ART DIRECTOR:
Richard Turley
CLIENT: Guardian UK
MEDIUM: Ink, digital

P. 121
ART DIRECTOR:
Sam Solomon
CLIENT: American
Way Magazine
MEDIUM: Ink, digital

P. 285
CLIENT:
Totoro Forest Project
MEDIUM: Ink

SILVER
P. 300
ART DIRECTOR:
Lisa Lapointe
CLIENT:
Penguin Canada
MEDIUM: Ink, digital

P. 507
ART DIRECTORS:
Kim Bost, Brian Rea
CLIENT:
The New York Times
MEDIUM: Ink, digital

P. 506
ART DIRECTOR:
Brian Morgan
CLIENT: The Walrus
MEDIUM: Ink, digital

AI TATEBAYASHI
8835 Elmhurst Ave. #4B
Elmhurst, NY 11373
917-821-4329
ai@miniai.com
www.miniai.com

P. 454
MEDIUM:
Gouache

JEFFREY STEWART TIMMINS
c/o Shannon Associates
568 Ossington Ave. 1st Fl.
Toronto M6G 3T5, Canada
416-535-9077
studio@goutwort.ca

P. 509
ART DIRECTOR: Jeffrey
Stewart Timmins
CLIENT: ARC Institute
MEDIUM: Ink, water-
color, aftereffects

ADRIAN TOMINE
illustration@adrian-tomine.com
www.adrian-tomine.com

P. 122
ART DIRECTOR OF COVERS:
Françoise Mouly
CLIENT:
The New Yorker

JUNICHI TSUNEOKA
9407 21st Ave. SW
Seattle, WA 98106
206-388-5052
studio@stubbornsideburn.com
stubbornsideburn.com

P. 219
ART DIRECTOR:
Junichi Tsuneoka
CLIENT: Showbox
MEDIUM: Silkscreen

POL TURGEON
5187 Jeanne-Mance #3
Montreal, Quebec H2V 4K2, Canada
514-273-8329
pol@polturgeon.com
www.polturgeon.com

P. 222
ART DIRECTOR:
Pol Turgeon
CLIENT:
Society of Illustrators
MEDIUM: Mixed

P. 223
CLIENT:
Society of Illustrators

P. 224
ART DIRECTORS:
Andre Barbe,
Renaud Doucet
CLIENT:
Barbe & Doucet
MEDIUM: Mixed

RICHARD TUSCHMAN
Richard Tuschman Images
8420 Islesworth Ct. #15305
Sarasota, FL 34243
rt@richardtuschman.com
www.richardtuschman.com

P. 410
ART DIRECTOR:
Robbin Gourley
CLIENT: Farrar,
Straus and Giroux
MEDIUM:
Mixed, digital

JONATHAN TWINGLEY
615 W 172nd St. #53
New York, NY 10032
917-613-2144
twingley@verizon.net
www.twingley.com

P. 123
ART DIRECTOR:
Larry Gendron
CLIENT: The Deal
MEDIUM:
Acrylic on canvas

MARK ULRIKSEN
841 Shrader St.
San Francisco, CA 94117
415-387-0170
mark@markulriksen.com
www.markulriksen.com

P. 124
ART DIRECTOR OF COVERS:
Françoise Mouly
CLIENT:
The New Yorker

P. 125
ART DIRECTOR OF COVERS:
Françoise Mouly
CLIENT:
The New Yorker
MEDIUM:
Acrylic on paper

JACK UNRUH
8138 Santa Clara Dr.
Dallas, TX 75218
214-324-2720
jack@jackunruh.com
www.jackunruh.com

P. 126
ART DIRECTOR:
T.J. Tucker
CLIENT:
Texas Monthly
MEDIUM:
Ink, watercolor

P. 127
ART DIRECTOR:
Caroline Jackson
CLIENT:
New York Magazine
MEDIUM:
Ink, watercolor

P. 411
ART DIRECTOR:
D.J. Stout
CLIENT: Texas A & M
MEDIUM:
Ink, watercolor

SILVER
P. 428
MEDIUM:
Ink, watercolor

FRANCIS VALLEJO
1130 Greensboro Ln.
Mailbox 1090
Sarasota, FL 34234
313-258-3294
fvallejo.illustration@gmail.com

P. 510
ART DIRECTOR:
Michael Meier
CLIENT: Rotopol Pree
MEDIUM: Ink, digital

WALTER VASCONCELOS
c/o Frank Sturges Reps
142 W Winter St.
Delaware, OH 43015
740-369-9702
frank@sturgesrep.com
www.sturgesrep.com

P. 286
ART DIRECTOR:
Steve Gabor
CLIENT: Baseman
Printing, Salvator
Coe & Gabor
MEDIUM: Digital

JON VERMILYEA
204 Greenpoint Ave. #1L
Brooklyn, NY 11222
917-685-7375
jonvermilyea@gmail.com
www.jonvermilyea.com

P. 412
ART DIRECTOR:
Jacob Covey
CLIENT:
Fantagraphics Books
MEDIUM: Ink, digital

BRUCE WALDMAN
18 Westbrook Rd.
Westfield, NJ 07090
908-337-3432
bruce@brucewaldman.com
www.brucewaldman.com

P. 225
ART DIRECTOR:
Christine Morrison
CLIENT: Technical
Analysis of Stocks
and Commodities
MEDIUM: Monoprint

MICHAEL WANDELMAIER
info@wandelmaier.com
www.wandelmaier.com

P. 455
MEDIUM:
Graphite on Bristol,
digital coloring

SAM WEBER
268 Nassau Ave. #3L
Brooklyn, NY 11222
917-374-3373
sam@sampaints.com

GOLD
P. 42
ART DIRECTOR:
Nicholas Blechman
CLIENT: The New York
Times Book Review
MEDIUM:
Watercolor, digital

P. 128
ART DIRECTOR:
Brian Rea
CLIENT: The New York
Times Op-Ed Page
MEDIUM: Ink

P. 226
ART DIRECTOR:
Anthony Swaneveld
CLIENT:
Soulpepper Theater
MEDIUM: Watercolor,
acrylic, digital

P. 227
ART DIRECTOR:
Anthony Swaneveld
CLIENT:
Soulpepper Theatre
MEDIUM: Watercolor,
acrylic, digital

P. 228
ART DIRECTOR:
Anthony Swaneveld
CLIENT:
Soulpepper Theatre
MEDIUM: Watercolor,
acrylic, digital

P. 287
CLIENT:
Totoro Forest Project
MEDIUM:
Watercolor, digital

P. 414
ART DIRECTOR:
Angela Rufino
CLIENT:
DC/Vertigo Comics
MEDIUM:
Watercolor, digital

P. 415
ART DIRECTOR:
Irene Gallo
CLIENT: Tor Books
MEDIUM:
Watercolor, digital

KYLE T. WEBSTER
2418 Lyndhurst Ave.
Winston-Salem, NC 27103
336-253-4612
kyle@kyletwebster.com
www.kyletwebster.com

P. 229
ART DIRECTOR:
Troy Tyner
CLIENT: Triad Stage
MEDIUM: Mixed

GORDON WIEBE
c/o Magnet Reps
1685 H St. #219
Blaine, WA 98230
866-390-5656
cora@magnetreps.com
www.magnetreps.com

P. 232
ART DIRECTORS:
Meryl Stebel,
Nara Gumbs
CLIENT:
The Partnership for
a Drug Free America
MEDIUM: Mixed

RICHARD WILLIAMS
112 Ruskin Ave.
Syracuse, NY 13207
315-488-6164
rwilli5@twcny.rr.com

P. 129
ART DIRECTOR:
Sam Viviano
CLIENT:
MAD Magazine
MEDIUM:
Oil on canvas

NATE WILLIAMS
c/o Magnet Reps
1685 H St. #219
Blaine, WA 98230
866-390-5656
cora@magnetreps.com
www.magnetreps.com

P. 288
CLIENT:
Urban Outfitters
MEDIUM:
Mixed, digital

P. 230
ART DIRECTOR:
Kevin Salem
CLIENT:
Little Monster Records
MEDIUM:
Mixed, digital

P. 231
ART DIRECTOR:
Tristan Rault
CLIENT: Museo de
Arte Latinoamericano
de Buenos Aires
MEDIUM: Mixed, digital

KATE T. WILLIAMSON
917-566-1650
katetower@gmail.com
www.katetwilliamson.com

P. 511
CLIENT: Princeton
Architectural Press
MEDIUM: Watercolor,
ink, digital

ALAN WITSCHONKE
67 Everett St.
Natick, MA 01760
508-653-1607
alanwits@comcast.net
www.alanwitschonke.com

P. 416
ART DIRECTOR:
Lesley Ehlers
CLIENT: Mikaya Press
MEDIUM: Dyes

P. 417
ART DIRECTOR:
Lesley Ehlers
CLIENT: Mikaya Press
MEDIUM: Dyes

MATTHEW WOOD
1911 Pepper Dr.
Altadena, CA 91001
626-644-6528
morewood@gmail.com

P. 418
ART DIRECTOR:
Tom Knechtel
CLIENT: ACCD
MEDIUM:
Egg Tempera

JULIA WOOLF
27 West St.
Faversham, Kent ME13 7JP, England
(01144) 1795-536964
juliawolf@earthlink.net

P. 289
CLIENT:
Totoro Forest Project
MEDIUM: Digital

TED WRIGHT
4237 Hansard Ln.
Hillsboro, MI 63050
314-607-9901
twrightart@aol.com

P. 512
ART DIRECTOR:
Jeff McLean
CLIENT: Ambleside
MEDIUM:
Pen & ink, digital

EUGENE YELCHIN
1555 Greenleaf Canyon Rd.
Topanga, CA 90290
310-455-3911
eugeneyelchin@yahoo.com

P. 419
ART DIRECTOR:
Martha Rago
CLIENT: HarperCollins
MEDIUM: Gouache,
ink on paper

CRAIG ZUCKERMAN
109 Carthage Rd.
Scarsdale, NY 10583
914-725-6004
cpz@bestweb.net

P. 233
ART DIRECTOR:
Gabriel Mattar
CLIENT: Funk Eyeware
MEDIUM:
Photoshop, 3D

ART DIRECTORS

PARSONS BFA IN ILLUSTRATION

Congratulates

The Society of Illustrators
2009 Zankel Scholar Finalist

KATIE TURNER, Class of 2010

See more of Katie's work at www.katieturner.net

A pioneer in the field of illustration since the early 1900s, Parsons The New School for Design continues to set the pace in the world of visual communication.

PARSONS THE NEW SCHOOL FOR DESIGN

www.newschool.edu/illustration

GERALD AND CULLEN RAPP

420 Lexington Ave
Penthouse
New York, NY 10170

Ph 212 889 3337
Fx 212 889 3341
info@rappart.com

Beth Adams

Joseph Adolphe

Brian Ajhar

Raúl Allén

Philip Anderson

Shino Arihara

Brian Biggs

Stuart Briers

David M. Brinley

Nigel Buchanan

Lonnie Busch

Harry Campbell

Jonathan Carlson

Stephanie Dalton Cowan

Robert de Michiell

John S. Dykes

EAMO

Jan Feindt

Matthieu Forichon

Phil Foster

Anthony Freda

Mark Fredrickson

Arthur E. Giron

Asaf Hanuka

Peter Horjus

Peter Horvath

Celia Johnson

Douglas Jones

Federico Jordán

James Kaczman

J.D. King

Laszlo Kubinyi

Jerome Lagarrigue

PJ Loughran

Bernard Maisner

Hal Mayforth

Sean McCabe

Richard Mia

Bruce Morser

James O'Brien

Dan Page

Cara Petrus

John Pirman

Jean-Francois Podevin

Rafael Ricoy

Marc Rosenthal

Alison Seiffer

Seth

Whitney Sherman

Jeffrey Smith

Ryan Snook

James Steinberg

Sharon Tancredi

Elizabeth Traynor

Andy Ward

Anders Wenngren

Michael Witte

Noah Woods

Phil Wrigglesworth

Brad Yeo

THE ILLUSTRATION ACADEMY

summer 2010

Mark English, Doug Chayka, Jon Foster, John English, Sterling Hundley, Gary Kelley
Anita Kunz, Robert Meganck, C.F. Payne, George Pratt, Barron Storey, Brent Watkinson
Natalie Ascencios, Terry Brown, Francis Livingston, Jillian Tamaki, Sam Weber

MAY 31-JULY 16
Lecture Week:
June 21-25

WWW.ILLUSTRATIONACADEMY.COM

WHY ILLUSTRATION?

UNFORTUNATELY ILLUSTRATION IS *NOT* AT THE TOP OF THE LIST WHEN ART DIRECTORS ARE THINKING ABOUT *SOLVING* VISUAL PROBLEMS.

SURE THERE ARE THE DEVOTEES OUT THERE, PARTICULARLY ON THE EDITORIAL SIDE, BUT IT'S *RARE* TO FIND AN AD AGENCY ART DIRECTOR USING *ILLUSTRATION*.

THERE SEEMS TO BE A REAL *FEAR* AMONG ART DIRECTORS TO HIRE ILLUSTRATORS. THEY MAY THINK THEY'RE GIVING UP CREATIVE *CONTROL*, OR THINK THAT IT'S TOO *DIFFICULT* OR IT TAKES TOO LONG TO DO AN ILLUSTRATION. THAT'S WHERE THEY CAN BENEFIT FROM THE *EXPERIENCE* OF EDITORIAL ART DIRECTORS WHO HAVE EVEN *TIGHTER* DEADLINES.

§ WORKING WITH AN ILLUSTRATOR IS *NOT* DIFFICULT, GETTING VISUAL IDEAS FROM ILLUSTRATORS ISN'T A *COP-OUT*. WORKING IN PARTNERSHIP WITH AN ILLUSTRATOR CAN *BENEFIT* THE CLIENT AND CAREER OF *ANY* ART DIRECTOR.

§ WE BELIEVE PHOTOGRAPHY *CANNOT* REPLICATE THE IDEAS ILLUSTRATORS DREAM UP. THAT *NO* AMOUNT OF DIGITAL MANIPULATION CAN MANUFACTURE AN *IDEA*.

§ AND WE SEE TODAY'S COMMERCIAL PHOTOGRAPHY LOOKING ALL TOO MUCH THE *SAME*. WHEREAS ILLUSTRATION LOOKS AS *DIFFERENT* AS THE ARTISTS THEMSELVES.

§ EVERYONE CONSIDERS THEMSELVES A PHOTOGRAPHER, *ANYONE* CAN TAKE A PICTURE. *FEW* CAN DRAW OR PAINT ONE.

AND DRAUGHTSMANSHIP ISN'T ENOUGH. THE *TRUE* ILLUSTRATOR IS A VISUAL PROBLEM-SOLVER PAR EXCELLENCE. EACH BRINGS A *UNIQUE* PERSPECTIVE ON OUR WORLD, A PERSONAL *VISION* THAT IS TRANSLATED IN INK, PAINT OR PIXELS. AN *IDEA* THAT ECHOES OUR TIMES, AS *ORIGINAL* AS ORIGINAL GETS.

YOU CAN COUNT ON *ONE* HAND THE TRULY EXTRAORDINARY PHOTOGRAPHERS WORKING TODAY; YOU CAN *FILL* A BOOK WITH THE WORK OF TODAY'S ARTISTS. *ENJOY*.

3 x 3
The Magazine of Contemporary Illustration

Three by Three magazine and award annuals have been recognized for its content and design by The Society of Publication Designers, Applied Arts, Communication Arts and HOW International Design Annual and featured on the AIGA website and illustrationmundo.com podcasts.

WWW.3X3MAG.COM

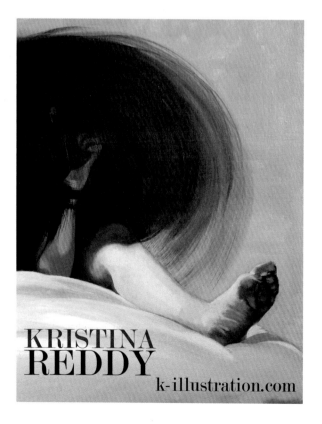

the illustration site

Adam McCauley
Gold Medal, Book

Leo Espinosa
Silver Medal,
Institutional

Nigel Buchanan
Silver Medal,
Institutional

Edel Rodriguez
Silver Medal,
Advertising

Hal Mayforth
Silver Medal, Uncommissioned

ILLUSTRATION
AT THE UNIVERSITY OF THE ARTS

TRADITIONAL
CONTEMPORARY
COMPREHENSIVE
PERSONALIZED

Rooted in the fundamentals of drawing and picture making for over 130 years, Illustration at the University of the Arts empowers students to choose their personal path – from cutting-edge digital to time-honored traditional.

Immersed in a collegial environment of mentorship and professionalism, and engaged in a time-tested curriculum, students work one-on-one with award-winning faculty.

The University's Richard C. von Hess Illustration Gallery provides students with invaluable insights through up close exposure to varied stylistic and conceptual approaches. The gallery is one of the nation's few contemporary professional illustration galleries.

UNIVERSITY OF THE ARTS ILLUSTRATION STUDENTS, FACULTY & ALUMNI OFFER CONGRATULATIONS TO...

FACULTY MEMBER **TIM O'BRIEN**
2009 Society of Illustrators Hamilton King Award Winner

ALUMNUS **ARNOLD ROTH**
2009 Society of Illustrators Hall of Fame Inductee

Illustration by Tom Leonard '77 (Illustration), Adjunct Professor

The University of the Arts
320 S. Broad Street
Philadelphia, PA 19102
215.717.6240
www.uartsillustration.com

3 1192 01492 0720